D1301833

"WITH A DEMONSTRATION OF THE SPIRIT AND OF POWER"

"With a Demonstration of the Spirit and of Power"

Seventh International Consultation of United and Uniting Churches

EDITED BY THOMAS F. BEST

Faith and Order Paper No. 195

WCC Publications, Geneva

Biblical quotations are taken from the New Revised Standard Version, except in the paper by Jerry Pillay where the New International Version has been used.

Cover design: Stephen Raw

ISBN 2-8254-1395-X

World Council of Churches
P.O. Box 2100, 150 route de Ferney
1211 Geneva 2, Switzerland
Website: http://www.wcc-coe.org

Printed in Switzerland

Table of Contents

vii Foreword *Bas Plaisier and Leo J. Koffeman*

xi Introduction *Thomas F. Best*

I. Report

3 Message from the Consultation

13 Information Release

II. Papers

UNITY

19 Unity: A Contribution from the Reformed Tradition
Martien E. Brinkman

31 The Ghanaian Ministry for London: A Case Study on Unity
Francis Amenu

39 The Impact of Unity: A Case Study
Leo J. Koffeman

MISSION

46 A Mission of Unity and a Unity of Mission: Perspectives in the Mission of United and Uniting Churches
Jerry Pillay

59 A Case Study in Mission: The United Church in Jamaica and the Cayman Islands
Norbert D. Stephens

69 A Case Study on the Relationship between Mission and Unity: The Uniting Church in Australia
Terence Corkin

IDENTITY

76 Earthen Vessels or God's Building? The Identity of United and Uniting Churches
David M. Thompson

99 Churches Uniting in Christ: A Case Study in Identity
Michael Kinnamon

105 A Case Study on Identity: The Communion of Churches in India
D.K. Sahu

III. Special Account

115 The Dutch Reformed Church Family in South Africa: Lessons Learned on the Way to Reunification
Piet Meiring

IV. Bible Studies

135 Unity, Mission, Identity: In Paul's Ephesus – and Now?
Jet den Hollander

144 Approaching Identity through Exile – a Welsh Perspective
Peter Cruchley-Jones

156 "What Kind of Fools Are We?": God's Wisdom in Our World Today
Bertrice Y. Wood

V. Sermons

163 The Search for Unity: The Task of the Church
John W. Gladstone

168 Homily on John 21:1-14
John A. Radano

173 The Imperative of Unity
Bas Plaisier

177 **Participants**

180 **Contributors**

Foreword

BAS PLAISIER AND LEO J. KOFFEMAN

It is a happy coincidence that this book is being published in 2004. For us, as the hosting churches of the seventh international consultation of United and Uniting churches held 12-18 September 2002 in Driebergen, Netherlands, the year 2004 has historic significance. As from 1 May 2004, our process of unification into one Protestant Church in the Netherlands will be completed. Together the Netherlands Reformed Church (NRC), the Reformed Churches in the Netherlands (RCN) and the Evangelical Lutheran Church in the Kingdom of the Netherlands (ELC) continue their existence – and, what is more vital, their ministry in this world.

For us this perspective was a major reason for inviting Faith and Order to organize the seventh consultation in the Netherlands. Whereas tensions were increasing in the final stage of our unification process, we hoped to find encouragement from the worldwide family of United and Uniting churches. At the same time, we were aware of some experiences of ours which might serve the continuing ecclesial and theological quest for the unity we seek. In September 2002, both expectations were met – and abundantly so! It was a privilege for us to host so many ecumenical friends.

The request to write a foreword to this publication of the Driebergen consultation offers us a welcome opportunity to present a modest update regarding recent developments in our country. Over the last eighteen months the three synods involved were able to take the required steps according to schedule. Final decisions were taken on 12 December 2003, and we are pleased to include below the Declaration on Unification signed that evening by representatives of the synods. (Church courts in the NRC and RCN still have to deal with formal appeals against these decisions, but we are confident that no further delay will be necessary – even though, after the completion of internal procedures, civil court cases could take a few more years.)

The Driebergen consultation focused on three key words: unity – identity – mission. More than we had expected, the completion of the unification process generated new interest in issues of identity and mission. In November 2003 a programmatic "profile" of the Protestant Church in the Netherlands was agreed upon. This will determine the ministries of the Protestant Church in the Netherlands. It says:

> The Protestant Church in the Netherlands recognizes its vocation for the coming years to give priority in its ministries to whatever contributes to:
> - the witness to the name of the Lord, here as well as worldwide;
> - the open communication between the church and its context;
> - the ministry of charity and justice;
> - the internal ecclesial conversations as a means of enrichment, encounter, and deepening of knowledge, understanding, commitment and engagement;
> - the education and training of the congregations for tomorrow's church and society;
> - an adequate exercise of the ministerial office.

That is how the Protestant Church in the Netherlands wants to be – according to the first sentence of its constitution – "a manifestation of the one, holy, catholic and apostolic church". In the short run, the focus will be especially on the first two of the six elements above. Within the church, in its synodical assemblies and beyond, a new discussion on the missionary aspects of the church will begin: what does it mean to witness, together with partner churches, to the name of Jesus Christ, both in a secularized country like the Netherlands and in other countries where we have long-lasting bonds with sister churches?

It seems that the time has come for a new and open communication with people today. Many of the historical burdens – prejudices as well as fair criticisms – which often hampered our witness in the past have fallen away. It is no long the exception when younger generations are curious about (or even unambiguously interested in!) what the gospel might mean today.

In the future we continue to count on the warm interest and the prayers of our sister churches, as we experienced this in Driebergen. May the Lord bless all of us!

March 2004

Declaration on Unification

Today, 12 December 2004,

the general synod of the Netherlands Reformed Church
the general synod of the Reformed Churches in the Netherlands
and the synod of the Evangelical Lutheran Church in the Kingdom of the Netherlands

decided to unite the churches which are entrusted to their care and guidance into the Protestant Church in the Netherlands.

We unite in believing that *our Lord Jesus Christ* himself prayed for the unity of his church, so that the world may believe in him.

The separate roads which our churches in the Netherlands have been following since the Reformation in the 16th century, and the two secessions in the 19th century, come together here.

In recent years the churches have been "together on the way" with the purpose of uniting. In decisions and declarations, and especially in accepting the church order of the Protestant Church in the Netherlands, our longing for unity has gradually taken shape.

We pray for renewal by *the Holy Spirit* and express

- our confidence that the Spirit will continue to lead his church;
- our desire to proclaim the name of our Lord and to give expression to his love and faithfulness in Dutch society;
- our hope that – where concerns continue to exist within the church – we may find each other in the name of our Lord;
- our willingness to continue seeking a growing visible unity of God's church in the future.

Soli Deo Gloria

[Provisional translation from the Dutch by Leo Koffeman]

Introduction

THOMAS F. BEST

What does visible unity look like? How can the churches' mission express their common faith and witness, rather than – as too often happens – promoting division in both church and community? What is the identity and calling of the church, in a world wary of institutions and all claims to truth? And, not least: How can the churches relate responsibly to one another, to other churches worldwide, and to their partners in mission and service?

Such were the questions which challenged the seventh international consultation of United and Uniting churches, meeting in Driebergen, Netherlands, 12-18 September 2002. The consultation gathered at the invitation of the *Samen op Weg* (Together on the Way) churches[1] in the Netherlands, churches then wrestling with the decision whether to commit themselves irreversibly to visible, structural union. Some fifty participants were present, representing almost sixty church and ecumenical bodies, including persons from United and Uniting churches, mission and specialized ministries (donor agency) partners, as well as local observers. These were joined by observers from the Roman Catholic and Orthodox churches.

The context of the meeting: global, local, historical

The meeting was set within a global and a local context. In inviting the consultation to meet in their country, the *Samen op Weg* churches were seeking to share with the worldwide family of United and Uniting churches their long experience on the way to church union in the Netherlands. At the same time they were hoping to learn from the experience of other union processes and united churches, and to receive their encouragement – and helpful critique. This exchange was fostered not only at the meeting itself but also through an extensive programme of church visits, with participants attending Sunday worship, getting to know church life in the Netherlands in the local parish context, and sharing ideas and experiences of church union directly with parishioners.

There was also an historical context for the meeting. For Driebergen was the latest in a series of such gatherings – at Bossey, Switzerland (1967);[2] Limuru, Kenya (1970);[3] Toronto, Canada (1975);[4] Colombo, Sri Lanka (1981);[5] Potsdam, GDR (1987);[6] and Ocho Rios, Jamaica, West Indies (1995)[7] – organized by the Faith and Order Commission of the World Council of Churches at the request, and on behalf, of the family of United and Uniting churches worldwide.[8] These meetings have been complemented by the surveys of church union negotiations begun under Faith and Order's auspices in 1927(!) and, from 1954, published by Faith and Order at 2-3 year intervals in *The Ecumenical Review*.[9] The consultation, then, was well aware of the United and Uniting churches' vision and ethos, and the achievements – and setbacks – which have marked the church union movement through its almost 200-year history.

Themes and programme of the consultation

The consultation themes of *unity*, *mission* and *identity* had been identified through long discussion with the United and Uniting churches themselves. Each topic was addressed in a major presentation, complemented by two case studies, bringing the voices of United and Uniting churches from the Netherlands, Ghana and the United Kingdom, South Africa, Jamaica, Australia, the United States and India. A special moment in the consultation came with a frank presentation on the Dutch Reformed Church in South Africa in its relation to apartheid. It was a story difficult for some to tell, and for others to hear: but it was told, and it was heard, and that telling and hearing became part of a healing process.

Bible studies brought key biblical texts on unity to speak to the churches in their search for unity today. These were complemented by sermons on unity texts in the consultation's opening and closing worship, and in one daily worship. Information sessions brought word of the latest developments in union activities, for example in Germany.

For this publication each contributor was given the opportunity to provide an "author's addendum", updating his or her text in light of developments since September 2002.

As an overarching theme the complex issue of relationships emerged: relationships among the United and Uniting churches themselves and between them and their mission and diaconal partners, as well as the Christian world communions. The consultation message, concise yet substantial, stresses the mutual support and accountability felt among the United and Uniting churches, and poses refreshingly direct questions to the churches, to their partners, and to the world communions alike.

The consultation appointed a continuation committee including Leo Koffeman, Sheila Maxey, D.K. Sahu, Robert Welsh and Londi Zulu to foresee, and oversee, further work on behalf of the United and Uniting churches worldwide.

Thanks

On behalf of the United and Uniting churches and Faith and Order, I am happy to express thanks to all those in the Netherlands who made the consultation such a memorable event: to Leo Koffeman as organizer in the local context; to the *Samen op Weg* churches which, as hosts for the event, provided staff and material support, as well as to Bas Plaisier and Leo Koffeman for contributing the foreword to this book on behalf of the now-united Protestant Church in the Netherlands; to the Maranathakerk, Driebergen, for hosting the consultation's opening and closing worships, as well as to Willem Timmerman, Arie van der Plas, Bas Plaisier, Eef Keuken and Evert Kuiken for providing leadership in those events; to the many congregations which received us for Sunday worship and for an introduction to local church life; and for those who organized and provided for the cultural excursion.

In addition thanks are due to the presenters, Bible study leaders, worship leaders, preachers, group leaders and, not least, drafters who provided leadership for the consultation itself. Special thanks are extended to Sheila Maxey who served as worship organizer for the consultation, and to the consultation planning group of Leo Koffeman, Sheila Maxey, V.S. Lall and Robert Welsh, which worked for almost three years to plan and organize the event in the international context.

We are deeply grateful to the Council for World Mission (CWM), London, which, through its Ecumenical Projects fund, provided major support for the consultation; to the Reformed Churches in the Netherlands and the United Reformed Church, CWM member churches which facilitated the funding process; and to all others who provided material support for the event.

Looking ahead: towards, through and beyond union

The search for unity has borne further fruit since the Driebergen consultation in 2002. Time fails for details – for these see the next edition of the church union survey – but, for example, notable steps towards visible unity have been taken by uniting churches in Wales and India, and significant work on ecclesiological issues is being done by the church union processes in South Africa and the United States.

And today, even as I write these lines, the three *Samen op Weg* churches are entering into their new identity, taking forward their lives and ministry as a single, United church: the Protestant Church in the Netherlands. We thank the churches, now one church, again for hosting the seventh international consultation of United and Uniting churches; we celebrate their courage and vision in bringing their long union process to completion; and we wish them Godspeed as they enter into their union, and blessings for the years ahead.

1 May 2004

NOTES

[1] That is, the Netherlands Reformed Church (NRC), the Reformed Churches in the Netherlands (RCN), and the Evangelical Lutheran Church in the Kingdom of the Netherlands (ELC).

[2] *Mid-Stream*, 6, 1967, report pp.10-15, notes from the discussion pp.16-22; German: see *Kirchenunionen und Kirchengemeinschaft*, hrsg. von Reinhard Groscurth, Frankfurt am Main, Otto Lembeck, 1971, report pp.115-21.

[3] *Mid-Stream*, 9, 1970, report pp.4-12, notes from the discussion pp.13-33; German: see *Kirchenunionen und Kirchengemeinschaft*, hrsg. von Reinhard Groscurth, Frankfurt am Main, Otto Lembeck, 1971, report pp.123-31, notes from the discussion pp.133-51.

[4] *Mid-Stream*, 14, 1975, report pp.541-63; see also *What Unity Requires*, Faith and Order Paper no. 77, WCC, 1976, pp.18-29. German: report, "Berufen, Christi Kreuz und Herrlichkeit zu bezeugen. Eine Botschaft der Konsultation von vereinigten Kirchen und Unionsausschüssen in Toronto", in *Ökumenische Rundschau*, 24, 4, Oktober 1975, pp.495-506.

[5] *Growing towards Consensus and Commitment*, Faith and Order Paper no. 110, WCC, 1981, report pp.1-35; see also *Unity in Each Place... In All Places...: United Churches and the Christian World Communions*, Michael Kinnamon ed., Faith and Order Paper no. 118, WCC, 1983, report pp.101-35. German: report, *Wachsen im Konsensus und in der Verpflichtung*, Colombo, 1981, Berlin, Kirchenkanzlei der Evangelischen Kirche der Union, 1982. See also *Called to be One in Christ: United Churches and the Ecumenical Movement*, Michael Kinnamon and Thomas F. Best eds, Faith and Order Paper no. 127, WCC, 1985.

[6] *Living Today towards Visible Unity: The Fifth International Consultation of United and Uniting Churches*, Thomas F. Best ed., Faith and Order Paper no. 142, WCC, 1988, report pp.1-20; German: see *Gemeinsam auf dem Weg zur sichtbaren Einheit*, hrsg. von Reinhard Groscurth, Berlin, Kirchenkanzlei der Evangelischen Kirche der Union, 1988, cf. pp.10-11,20-24,27-28.

[7] *Built Together: The Present Vocation of United and Uniting Churches (Ephesians 2:22)*, Thomas F. Best ed., Faith and Order Paper no. 174, WCC, 1995, report and letter from the director of Faith and Order, pp.6-31.

[8] Faith and Order is mandated "to provide opportunities for consultation among those whose churches are engaged in union negotiations or other specific efforts towards unity", bylaws of the Faith and Order Commission, 2, aim and functions, section g.

[9] H. Paul Douglas, *A Decade of Objective Progress in Church Unity: 1927-1936*, New York, Harper, 1937; Stephen Neill, *Towards Church Union 1937-1952: A Survey of Approaches to Closer Union Among the Churches*, Faith and Order Paper no. 11, London, published on behalf of the Faith and Order Commission by SCM Press, 1952; thereafter in *The Ecumenical Review (ER)*: 6, 3, April 1954; 8, 1, Oct. 1955; 9, 3, April 1957; 12, 2, Jan. 1960; 14, 3, April 1962; 16, 4, July 1964; F&Order Paper 47, *ER*, 18, 3, July 1966; F&O Paper 52, 20, 3, July 1968; F&O Paper 56, 22, 3, July 1970; F&O Paper 64, 24, 3, July 1972; F&O Paper 68, 26, 2, April 1974; F&O Paper 78, 28, 3, July 1976; F&O Paper 87, 30, 3, July 1978; F&O Paper 101, 32, 3, July 1980; 34, 4, Oct. 1982; F&O Paper 122, 36, 4, Oct. 1984; F&O Paper 133, 38, 4, Oct. 1986; F&O Paper 146, 41, 2, April 1989; F&O Paper 154, 44, 1, Jan. 1992; F&O Paper 169, 47, 1, Jan. 1995; F&O Paper 176, 49, 2, April 1997; F&O Paper 186, 52, 1, Jan. 2000; F&O Paper 192, 54, 3, July 2002.

I

Report

Message from the Consultation

"With a Demonstration of the Spirit and of Power" (1 Cor. 2:4):
The Life and Mission of the United and Uniting Churches

I. United and Uniting churches: context and challenge

Greetings to you in the name of Jesus Christ from sisters and brothers at the seventh international consultation of United and Uniting churches!

Our gathering, which was held at Driebergen in the Netherlands, took place at a moment of considerable promise and peril. The consultation began on 11 September 2002, the first anniversary of the devastating attacks in the United States of America and a week after the close of the World Summit on Sustainable Development in South Africa. Part way through our meeting, peace talks aimed at ending nineteen years of civil war in Sri Lanka got underway in Thailand.

These events reminded us, first, of the astonishing interdependence of the *oikoumene* (the whole inhabited earth). Steps towards peace in south Asia give encouragement to similar efforts in Northern Ireland or the Congo. Conversely, threats of war from the US undercut Muslim-Christian relations in the Philippines and raise the price of oil in Southern Africa; economic decisions made in Frankfurt or New York may well widen the gap between rich and poor and contribute to poverty in Lusaka or Chennai; ecological destruction and the spread of AIDS anywhere threaten the future of people everywhere.

Christians who identify themselves with God's work of unity, we recognized, should be particularly sensitive to forces of division and reconciliation in the world and particularly aware of the even-more-intense interdependence of the body of Christ. Beyond that, our shared identity as United and Uniting churches means that we have a special claim on one another. If the United Church of Zambia struggles with the burden of foreign debt and the AIDS pandemic, then their struggle must impact the mission agenda of the United Church of Christ in the United States. If the Evangelical Church of the Union in Germany wrestles with discrimination against foreign workers, their wrestling must figure prominently in the prayer life of the Church of South India. If poverty is a pressing issue for the United Church in Jamaica and the Cayman Islands, then it must be so as well for the United Church of Christ in Japan. In a religiously pluralistic world, the witness of the Church of Bangladesh in the midst of Muslim neighbours should be instructive for the Evangelical Church of Czech Brethren.

The historical context of the consultation reminded us, secondly, of how urgent it is that we witness to the reconciling love of God made known in Christ. In the face of such apparent fragmentation, the church must witness – by what it *does* and what it *is* – to the wholeness of God. In a time when talk of war is so pervasive, the church must witness to the peace of God. At a moment when the powers of the world seem to lack the capacity for self-criticism, even our willingness to confess our brokenness is a witness to the sovereignty of God. Unity is not simply a distant ideal or a pious hope; it is a divine gift that can be lived out, however partially, here and now.

Our prayer at the consultation was that our churches, timid and fractured as they often are, would be empowered by the Spirit, and thereby witness to God's power that tears down walls of hostility and brings together those who once were enemies. The meeting's theme, "With a demonstration of the Spirit and of power", from Paul's first letter to the Corinthians, kept this prayer before us throughout our days together.

II. The unity and diversity of United and Uniting churches

There is much to celebrate since the sixth consultation of United and Uniting churches in 1995, including the formation of the racially mixed Uniting Presbyterian Church in Southern Africa (1999); the commitment to create the communion of churches in India, signifying an even closer bond of shared confession, witness and service among the Church of North India, the Church of South India, and the Mar Thoma Church (1999); the union of the United Reformed Church in the United Kingdom and the Congregational Union of Scotland (2000); and the inauguration of a substantive covenant among nine US denominations, known as Churches Uniting in Christ (2002). A full report on these and other church union developments can be found in the latest "Survey of Church Union Negotiations" (*The Ecumenical Review*, July 2002).

These churches, like others at the consultation, share a self-understanding shaped by an act of union or covenant; but, beyond that, they manifest extraordinary diversity. Some trace their history to the union of Reformed and Lutheran churches in 19th-century Germany; some are unions of Free and Reformed churches in North America and Europe; some represent the union of former mission churches, including Anglicans, in Africa, Asia, the Caribbean and the Pacific. Recent decades have seen a growth in covenant relationships that maintain confessional identities while forming a new whole that is greater than the sum of the parts.

Participants in the consultation agreed that a model of unity, if it is to deserve such a label, must be tangible enough to make a witness to the world, intense enough that those in it recognize their responsibility for one another, costly enough that churches are changed as a result of being in it, and intentional enough that the body of Christ is renewed through the sharing of gifts. We also agree, however, that no one model guarantees (or denies) such an outcome. The new models remind us to look for partners in unexpected places and to expect to be surprised by what God will do in our midst.

The tone of the consultation was actually a mixture of celebration for what God has done and repentance for what we have left undone. The Dutch unity process, *Samen op Weg* (Together on the Way), which served as a most gracious host for the meeting, exemplifies this tension. We were grateful for the opportunity to experience something of the life of Dutch churches and to enter into valuable and enjoyable discussions in local congregations. Many local Christians and church leaders with whom we spoke rejoiced in the reality or prospect of shared life among the Netherlands Reformed Church, the Reformed Churches in the Netherlands, and the Evangelical Lutheran Church in the Kingdom of the Netherlands. Others, however, expressed discouragement with the length and tedium of the effort. We could only offer the courage that comes from following God's calling and from knowing that they stand in the company of ecumenically minded Christians around the world, many of whom have successfully completed such a journey. We ask you to pray for and with these sisters and brothers in the Netherlands as they look towards full unification at the beginning of 2004.

III. Central issues of the consultation

The discussions at the consultation yielded a number of important insights and affirmations that are difficult to convey adequately in summary form. Among them:

- Authentic unity must directly address the issues that divide the human family in our particular settings (e.g. racism in the US, casteism in India, closure to refugees in Europe, and disparity of wealth in the Philippines). A uniting process that concentrates on traditional questions of faith and order without relating them to these issues of human division is responding only in part to the gift and command of unity in Christ.

- The gospel must be incarnate in each place, even as it transcends every culture. United and Uniting churches manifest catholicity by their adaptation to diverse local settings; but this must be coupled with a global vision manifest in intentional, intense relationships with churches in other cultures.
- Mission must be comprehensively defined as including *kerygma* (preaching), *koinonia* (fellowship), *diakonia* (service) and *leiturgia* (worship) – all understood as essential and inter-related dimensions of witness (*marturia*) to God's reign.
- Unity demands such qualities as mutual trust and mutual accountability and responsibility. Indeed, the presence of these is a measure of the "success" of the union. Participants spoke of a "spirituality of renunciation" that dares let go of cherished identity markers in order to receive a fuller identity through oneness in Christ. It is our experience that, again and again, we have been led to the foot of the cross, discovering there our true identity as followers of one who emptied himself that we might have fuller life. For this reason, we believe that the "burden of proof" is not on those who unite but on those who persist in division.
- It is important for United churches to remember and celebrate the time of union in order to keep fresh the uniting identity. Being "simply another denomination" is always a danger for these churches. For example, the Protestant Church in Baden has recently celebrated the 175th anniversary of its union, using this occasion for renewal of its commitment to mission and to a wider sense of the unity of the church.

At the heart of our discussions, as these examples indicate, was a concern to explore the inter-relatedness of unity, mission and identity. Previous consultations in this series have asked whether there is a distinctive witness made by United and Uniting churches and whether there is evidence that unity enhances mission. The answer, we must acknowledge, is mixed; but we note, for example, that the Church of South India considerably increased its membership in its first fifty years, and the United Church of Zambia has played a vital role in building a new nation. We remain convinced that *dis*unity is an impediment to mission, and that the very fact of being united in one body is a witness to the reconciling power of God. Nevertheless, the search for ecclesial unity can never be an end in itself. Without a constant focus on the imperative of mission, the search for unity will falter.

On the other hand, the search cannot be identified with one particular mission task. Colleagues from South Africa told us how Christians drawn together in the struggle against apartheid have experienced a slackening of mutual commitment since apartheid was abolished. The new relationships of unity need to be expressed in church life, worship and theology. In this respect, we share the hope of United States colleagues that Churches Uniting in Christ, emphasizing both eucharistic sharing and combating racism in the recently inaugurated covenant, will demonstrate the credibility of church reconciliation in everyday life.

This consultation has reaffirmed that the gift of resurrection and new life is the heart of our being as United and Uniting churches, celebrated as we gather at the Lord's table, made real as we seek to live God's unity by combating violence, racism and economic injustice. We have discovered in our various settings that a willingness to give away treasured but separate identities has helped us to receive the gift of God's superabundant generosity. Our faces are set to God's far horizon. There can be no turning back. What has been achieved is as nothing compared with what God has in store. Until all God's people, in all their amazing diversity, experience God's reconciling love we will remain a people on pilgrimage.

IV. Questions and recommendations to specific constituencies

A. To United and Uniting churches

Through this letter we, representatives of United and Uniting churches from around the world gathered in Driebergen, invite you to join the conversation outlined above. What are the issues of division and signs of reconciliation in your situation? Has your identity as a United or Uniting church strengthened your witness with regard to these issues? The papers presented at the consultation may be of use as your church reflects on these questions. Responses (which we strongly encourage!) may be sent to the WCC's Commission on Faith and Order, which continues to serve as a point of contact for United and Uniting churches.

There are many aspects of church life which can strengthen and encourage the church union process, or enrich the lives of churches already united. One example is joint theological education as undertaken by the United Church in Jamaica and the Cayman Islands even before its union (as well as by other Jamaican churches), with faculty and students exploring together the faith, worship life and witness of the still-divided churches. This promoted both an understanding of the wholeness of the nascent United church and a respect for its component parts, training a generation of pastors for service in a united, rather than a divided, church. We commend this model for wider adoption.

The sharing of experience can be crucially important in nurturing United churches and union processes. All sharing among the still-divided denominations and their congregations should be encouraged;

but the most effective is a focused, official sharing of the churches' worship, fellowship, witness and service. A good example is the sharing of worship materials and the joint preparation of eucharistic liturgies through the US Consultation on Church Union (Churches Uniting in Christ). Creative sharing at the international level is expressed in another way in the special relationship between two United churches, the United Church of Christ [USA] and the Evangelical Church of the Union [Germany]. We commend such sharing and the development of such relationships within the family of United and Uniting churches.

B. To the international mission partners of United and Uniting churches

We give thanks for those international mission boards and agencies which over the past forty years have restructured their organizations, creating a common pool of resources (not only financial) to which all contribute and in the allocation of which both givers and receivers make decisions together. We welcome the development of church-to-church relationships through which there is authentic partnership, including mutual sharing of resources, transparency, and mutual accountability and responsibility. We celebrate the emphasis on "mission to six continents", for example Ghanaians helping to shape mission life in the United Reformed Church in the London area and Indonesian teachers contributing to Philippine church life through ecumenical volunteer programmes.

At the same time, we recognize that even in the most radically restructured organizations there can still be a tension between what mission bodies wish to support and what their partner churches regard as mission priorities. In this way, unequal power relations between churches (especially churches in the South) and mission agencies can be perpetuated. This means that indirectly the agency sets the agenda of the churches, rather than the other way round, thereby distorting the missional identity of churches in both North and South.

Since our consultation affirmed the inseparable link between mission and unity, we celebrated the ways in which international bodies have, in many places, contributed to an ecumenical sense of mission. We are also aware, however, that "mission" and "ecumenical relations" are often handled separately in churches and agencies, thus undercutting even the best intentions.

Another problem is that historical ties often determine contemporary mission relationships, which means that some churches have a plethora of partners while others, facing the same challenges, have few if any. Sometimes mission bodies relate to only one part of a united church, thus fostering fragmentation. Sometimes United churches are tempted to be less than transparent in their dealings with multiple mission partners. Historical mission links should not be ignored, but they do need to be reviewed in order to address these issues.

With these issues in mind, we invite our mission partners to join the discussion of this consultation. Specifically, we ask you to think with us about the following questions: How can international mission relationships best be shaped, or reshaped, so that they facilitate authentic mission by each church in its own context? Are there ways that mission and unity can be held together more fully and effectively? How can international mission agencies cooperate more fully with one another in order to enable more effective local mission? Responses to these questions (which we strongly encourage!) can be sent to the Commission on Faith and Order through which we all can continue the dialogues.

C. To the general secretaries of the Christian world communions

Participants in the consultation are convinced that United and Uniting churches and Christian world communions can be and, in many cases, are mutually helpful colleagues in the work of the ecumenical movement. Because of this conviction, we wish to offer gifts we have received through the experience of union, to enlist your help, and to ask you to explore some questions with us.

Through the act of uniting, and with the guidance of the Spirit, we have received important insights about what it means to be "church". For example, some of our communions have discovered that infant/child and believers' baptism are not mutually exclusive, but complementary expressions of grace. The gift is in living the unity, not in inhabiting the past. We believe that we have much to offer from our experience to churches which are seeking to unite, and to world communions as you wrestle with issues which continue to divide us as Christians. We hope that we might work with you so that these gifts can be shared among ourselves (for we have no permanent institutional form beyond this consultation) and with those who are setting out on the road to unity.

One area where we certainly need your help has to do with new divisions in the body of Christ. We hope that the Christian world communions discourage divisions not only within their confessional families but within United churches. Should any group seek to secede from a United church, they should not be received by any world communion. This is not a theoretical matter. For example, you will be aware that twenty-three years after the Church of North India was formed in 1970, a group in the diocese of Eastern Himalayan broke away while still claiming to be the united Church of North India. We ask that Christian world communions reflect carefully on the implications of recognizing such groups as members, both in light of their own self-understanding as world communions and of their involvement in the one ecumenical movement. We commend the practice of some world communions of discussing such applications with other churches, including United churches, in the country concerned before decisions are taken.

We hope that as Christian world communions you will proclaim loudly your own commitment to unity and encourage dialogues and programmes that will lead to better ecumenical relations at all levels. We trust that you will do all you can to enable and support local churches that are engaged in a quest for new united identity.

Finally, difficulties are created for some of our churches by the proselytizing behaviour of some Christian bodies which do not belong to Christian world communions, but also by some churches which are part of world communions. We hope that you will bring pressure to bear on the latter, and encourage the former, to cooperate with United church partners.

There are several questions on which it would be good to reflect. United and Uniting churches, for example, emphasize adaptation to diverse local contexts rather than transcontextual confessional unity and the importance of transformation rather than confessional continuity. Some United churches find that affiliation with more than one world communion can be burdensome, even divisive. We welcome (even strongly encourage) direct conversation between representatives of United and Uniting churches and representatives of Christian world communions, perhaps facilitated by Faith and Order, on these and other issues.

D. To the Commission on Faith and Order of the World Council of Churches

We rejoice that by their very nature United and Uniting churches are bound closely to the work of the World Council of Churches, including the Faith and Order Commission which has provided both pastoral understanding and theological sustenance for our journeys. With this in mind, we ask that Faith and Order help us in further theological reflection on our experience as United and Uniting churches, most particularly in our ecclesiological self-understanding, and in our eucharistic experience as churches.

On the other hand, we believe that we have developed considerable expertise in the joys and difficulties of journeying towards unity, and would willingly make that expertise available to any churches which might benefit from it. We would be pleased to work with Faith and Order in order to share our ecumenical experience.

The participants in Driebergen are grateful to Faith and Order for all the commission has done to make this seventh consultation of United and Uniting churches such a significant event, and wish also to record our thanks to the Council for World Mission for their encouragement and generous financial support.

V. Conclusion: moving forward together

The United and Uniting churches meeting in Driebergen, at this moment of promise and peril, have affirmed their commitment to one another, as churches committed to the continuing search for unity. They have also affirmed the considerable, indeed surprising, diversity found within this family of churches, a diversity born of their attempts to be effective and faithful signs of God's reconciliation within their own contexts. They seek bonds of sharing and support, both spiritual and material, which can sustain their common life and strengthen them when they become weary. They look together to the Source of their faith and life, longing to be a sign, to both church and world, of the power of the gospel to unite that which is divided and to reconcile that which is estranged. Together they hope to experience, and to be, truly "a demonstration of the Spirit and of power".

Churches and church union processes represented at the consultation

Arnoldshainer Conference [Germany]
Christian Church (Disciples of Christ) [USA]
Church of Bangladesh
Church of Christ in Thailand
Church of England
Church of North India
Church of South India
Churches Uniting in Christ (CUIC) [USA]
Church Unity Commission (CUC) [South Africa]
Communion of Churches in India
Dutch Reformed Church [South Africa]
Ecumenical Partnership (Disciples of Christ/United Church of Christ) [USA]
ENFYS: The Covenanted Churches in Wales
Evangelical Church in Baden
Evangelical Church in Germany
Evangelical Church in Hessen and Nassau
Evangelical Church of the Church Province of Saxony
Evangelical Church of Czech Brethren
Evangelical Church of the Union [Germany]
Evangelical Lutheran Church in the Kingdom of the Netherlands

Evangelical Lutheran Church in Namibia
Evangelical Presbyterian Church, Ghana
Form of Cooperative Ventures [Aotearoa/New Zealand]
Mar Thoma Syrian Church of Malabar [India]
Methodist Church of Southern Africa
Netherlands Reformed Church
Philippine Independent Church
Presbyterian Church of Ghana
Presbyterian Church of New Zealand
Reformed Church in the Netherlands
Scottish Church Initiative for Union (SCIFU)
Scottish Episcopal Church
United Church in Jamaica and the Cayman Islands
United Church of Christ [USA]
United Church of Christ in Japan
United Church of Christ in the Philippines
United Church of Zambia
United Congregational Church of Southern Africa
United Evangelical Church – Anglican Communion in Angola
United Reformed Church [UK]
Uniting Church in Australia
Uniting Presbyterian Church in Southern Africa
Uniting Protestant Churches in the Netherlands (the *Samen op Weg* or "Together on the Way" Churches)

Christian world communions represented as observers

A. CWCs which include United and Uniting churches:
   Anglican Consultative Council
   Disciples Ecumenical Consultative Council
   Lutheran World Federation
   World Alliance of Reformed Churches
B. Ecumenical Patriarchate
C. Roman Catholic Church

International mission partners of United and Uniting churches represented

Council for World Mission (CWM)
Commission on World Mission and Evangelism, WCC
Mission and Evangelism Team, WCC
Netherlands Missionary Council

International theological commissions represented

Faith and Order Commission, WCC

Theological, material and organizational support for the consultation

Council for World Mission (CWM)
Faith and Order Commission, WCC
Uniting Protestant Churches in the Netherlands (the *Samen op Weg* or "Together on the Way" churches)

Information Release
23 September 2002

United and Uniting churches call for unity, dialogue with partners

The worldwide family of United and Uniting churches, meeting in Driebergen, Netherlands, 11-19 September 2002, has challenged all churches to renew their commitment to visible unity, and called for increased dialogue with mission partners and denominational church structures.

In an honest, self-critical meeting "full of spirit and hope for the future", United and Uniting churches explored the inter-relation of unity, mission and identity. Presentations on these topics were complemented by case studies and reports from unions and union processes around the world, workshops on theological and practical issues facing the churches today, and intensive encounters with *Samen op Weg* (Together on the Way), the church union process in the Netherlands which hosted the meeting (the process links two Reformed churches and one Lutheran church hoping for full unity by early 2004).

The meeting brought together representatives of more than forty-five United churches and church union processes, observers from mission partners and Christian world communions which include United churches, and observers from the Orthodox and Roman Catholic churches.

Opening worship and a closing eucharistic service were held in a local United congregation; daily worship, including challenging Bible studies, helped develop the consultation theme, "With a Demonstration of the Spirit and of Power" (1 Cor. 2:4).

Rather than a conventional report, the consultation issued a "concise, yet substantial" message reflecting the United and Uniting churches' distinctive identity and commitments, and inviting a range of partners (theological, missional, material and historical) into dialogue on matters which unite – and sometimes threaten to divide – them.

Participants agreed that a model of unity must be "tangible enough to make a witness to the world, intense enough that those in it recognize their responsibility for one another, costly enough that churches are changed as a result of being in it, and intentional enough that the body of Christ is renewed through the sharing of gifts".

The actual *form* of unity may vary considerably according to local circumstances, as was emphasized by churches coming from settings as diverse as Zambia, the Netherlands, South Africa, Jamaica, United States, India, Germany and the Philippines.

But whatever its form, "authentic unity must directly address the issues that divide the human family in our particular settings. A uniting process that concentrates on traditional questions of faith and order without relating them to these issues of human division is responding only in part to the gift and command of unity in Christ."

Participants noted that unity does not automatically lead to more effective mission, and some spoke frankly of their churches' need to be more effective in their witness to the transforming and reconciling power of the gospel. But, they agreed, it is clear that "*dis*unity is an impediment to mission, and that the very fact of being united in one body is a witness to the reconciling power of God".

Mission, which may also take diverse forms according to the local situation, must be understood broadly, "as including *kerygma* (preaching), *koinonia* (fellowship), *diakonia* (service) and *leiturgia* (worship) – all understood as essential and inter-related dimensions of witness (*marturia*) to God's reign".

Participants affirmed that the identity of United and Uniting churches is rooted in "a 'spirituality of renunciation' that dares let go of cherished identity markers in order to receive a fuller identity through oneness in Christ". This conviction gained special force in light of the church union experience in Netherlands, where "many local Christians and church leaders with whom we spoke rejoiced in the reality or prospect of shared life... Others, however, expressed discouragement with the length and tedium of the effort."

Recognizing the courage of the Dutch churches in pressing forward, and in light of their own experience of union, participants were quick to affirm the bold insistence of their hosts "that the 'burden of proof' is not on those [churches] who unite but on those who persist in division".

The consultation message calls for friendly but frank dialogues among United and Uniting churches, and between them and a series of partners. The *United and Uniting churches* themselves are asked to reflect together on "issues of division and signs of reconciliation" in their own contexts, and on whether the fact of union has actually strengthened their witness locally.

The United and Uniting churches recognize gratefully that their *mission partners* have sought new and mutually accountable forms of mission. Nevertheless, "unequal power relations... can be perpetuated", and the message calls for an open dialogue on how "international mission relationships [can] best be shaped, or reshaped, so that they facilitate authentic mission by each church in its own context".

Through their constituent churches, each United church or church union process finds itself related to two or more *Christian world communions*. These relationships can be a source of strength, but may invite a continuing denominationalism within a United church, or hamper efforts towards union. The message calls for direct, open conversations on these sensitive – and potentially controversial – issues.

In their life and work, participants affirmed, the United and Uniting churches are "longing to be a sign, to both church and world, of the power of the gospel to unite that which is divided and to reconcile that which is estranged. Together they hope to experience, and to be, truly 'a demonstration of the Spirit and of power'."

The consultation was the seventh in a series organized by the Faith and Order Commission of the World Council of Churches, which promotes theological dialogue and common action among the United and Uniting churches on issues which divide them. It was supported by the London-based Council for World Mission, which promotes new models of mission based on just sharing of resources among churches.

Background

United churches are those formed from unions across or within confessional families (most often involving Reformed, Congregationalist, Lutheran, Methodist, Disciples, Anglicans, and occasionally Church of the Brethren and others). The earliest union was formed in about 1817 in Germany; the most recent in 2000 and 2002 [now 2004 – ed.]. United churches have pioneered in overcoming several historic points of division among the churches, for example over infant and believers' baptism, and (where Anglicans have been involved) over the office of bishop. While very diverse, the United churches share a commitment to make unity both visible and effective in their lives.

Uniting churches are those moving towards union. In some contexts they are pursuing the classic model of structural integration of the divided churches to form a single ecclesial body. In other contexts churches are exploring other ways, such as covenant relationships, of making their unity in Christ visible and convincing, ranging from common worship to intensive partnerships for mission and service, to joint parishes. The next unions are forseen for 2003 in India and 2004 in the Netherlands.

(Some already-united churches identify themselves as "uniting" to stress their commitment to further union, an example being the Uniting Church in Australia.)

II

Papers

Unity: A Contribution from the Reformed Tradition

MARTIEN E. BRINKMAN

A lack of a sense of unity?

At first sight, from a historical point of view it seems rather absurd to speak about the contribution of the Reformed tradition to the unity of the church. For to this very day, Reformed people have taken pride in always having confessed their faith in their own way, *in tempore* and *in loco*.[1] The fact that their confessions of faith are always very much products of a certain time and place is not regarded by them as a disadvantage or admission of weakness, but rather as a point in their favour. This is the way, as they say, authentic confessing will always take place: it will always be contextually determined. Others, however, blame them because of their lack of any sense of unity beyond their own region and beyond their own time.

In his preface to a volume of contemporary *Reformed confessions*, Lukas Vischer, former director of the World Council of Churches' Commission on Faith and Order, quite explicitly links up with this historical tradition of confession:

> The churches belonging to the Reformed tradition have always been inclined to state their deepest convictions afresh in every new generation. They tend to regard the formulation of confessions of faith as part of the mandate of proclamation entrusted to the church.[2]

Unlike the Lutheran World Federation, whose members regard the Augsburg Confession as their doctrinal marker, the World Alliance of Reformed Churches (WARC) – as, for example, its counterparts the Baptist World Alliance and the World Methodist Council – has no one confession to which all its members subscribe, and which all agree should be used as a test of membership in the global family. It is, rather, up to each member church of the Alliance to adopt one or more confessions, to revise older standards or to compose new statements. This is why in the Reformed tradition there has never been a kind of "conclusion" to the doctrinal development – as we find, at least officially, in Lutheranism by way of the *Book of Concord* of 1580.[3]

Whereas the national Reformed churches often have a clearly confessional profile, the Reformed tradition as a whole not only lacks a hierarchical teaching ministry, but also something like a *hierarchia veritatum*, a hierarchy of truths (though a beginning of such had taken shape around Calvin's well-known distinction between fundamental and non-fundamental articles of faith[4]). But in general it may be said that in international ecumenical dialogues the "Reformed tradition" is a complicated discussion partner. It is difficult to "locate" us exactly as a discussion partner; our confessional background is too mobile for this.[5]

Two fundamental hermeneutical rules of the Reformed tradition

In this urge towards contextual witness one always encounters two important, basic assumptions which I like to indicate as fundamental rules of the hermeneutics of the Reformed tradition.

In the first place the central assumption of every biblical hermeneutics applies here: namely, that human understanding of the scriptures is always incomplete and can never grasp the meaning of God's word exhaustively. In the second place, this essential hermeneutic point of view implies that the concentration on one's own current situation of faith necessarily entails a restriction of one's own horizon of understanding.

In the actual approach of the confessional writings, however, these central hermeneutical points of view have often been disregarded. This disregard has, in a sense, already been implied in the intent to give a *summa scripturae* in a confession;[6] that very intent implies that this summary offers the most correct and pure interpretation of scripture.

This is also the reason why confessions of faith which by their names indicate a certain situational framework – as for example the *Confessio Scotica*, *Helvetica* and *Belgica* – have nevertheless, judged by their content, always been understood as being really universal, or catholic. To quote the WARC report "Towards a Common Testimony of Faith":

> In general, these confessions have combined a distinctly Reformed understanding of the gospel with the claim that this is a true expression of the apostolic teaching of the one catholic or universal church. While both universal and Reformed, our confessions have also attempted to relate the unchanging truths of the gospel to changing particulars of place and time and context.[7]

In spite of this pretension of universality (catholicity) one has, in fact, always realized the territorially confined character of one's own confession and never imposed it on other churches – except one's own missionary churches. One certainly has exported one's own particularity to them with a certain universal pretension. Therefore, one has every right now to defend the position that "one of the main reasons for the divided state of the Reformed family lies in the history of the missionary movement".[8]

Besides that of universality to particularity, another relation marked by tension is that between scripture and confession. In principle, the confession has always been regarded as a *norma normata* (an established norm), one established by scripture as a *norma normans* (the final and definite norm). This means that the relation between the confession and scripture is clearly one of dependence, the first upon the second.

The fact, however, that this relation is less obvious than it seems to be appears, for example, from the words of the late Dutch theologian Jan Koopmans. With regard to the relation between scripture and confession he speaks in his dissertation, which is one of the best studies on the Reformed concept of tradition, about a "vicious circle for the theological thinking of the churches of the Reformation". For in these churches the position is held that (on the one hand) no dogma is recognized by any church, unless it is grounded in scripture; while (on the other hand) no exegesis of scripture is accepted as correct, if it is in conflict with the dogma of the church. In fact this is tantamount to saying that dogma – we might also say here confession – may rightly be called a rule for exegesis.[9]

When one is unaware of this tension between scripture and confession, and naively time and again underscores the importance of the *sola scriptura*, one is always bound (this would at least be my thesis) to pay a high price for it: namely, either the doctrinalization of scripture or the biblicist foundation of dogma.[10] The evangelical movement nowadays quite often suffers from the former shortcoming, Lutheran and Calvinist orthodoxy from the latter.

In this connection the Reformed Dutch church historian Cornelis Augustijn points out that the subordination of the confession to the Bible always results, in time, in a subordination of the Bible to the confession. "In practice", he argues, "the aspect of the confession 'being the norm' will always prevail at the expense of the confession 'being established as the norm' by holy scripture (as *norma normata*). This is quite obvious, otherwise one would not need a confession. A confession, after all, is much easier to handle as a norm than scripture."[11]

The essential meaning of Augustijn's observations is that the Reformed *sola scriptura* can only really function when it is continually accompanied by another principle, namely the *ecclesia semper reformanda*. Justice has only been done to the *sola scriptura*, when the biblical interpretation of the church in its confession can also, in its turn, be criticized on the basis of scripture. To quote a WARC working paper on "Contemporary Questions Concerning the Sola Scriptura":

> It should be acknowledged that the Reformed churches in the past have claimed to have based their formulations of doctrine on scripture alone; in fact, they have always interpreted scripture within a certain (confessional, but also philosophical) tradition.

And hence, the working paper continues:

> The *ecclesia semper reformanda* surely requires the openness to judge our formulations in the light of our understanding of scripture, every time anew.[12]

The relation between old and new confessions

In spite of the fact that in the history of our churches the truth of the principle of the *sola scriptura* has frequently been suppressed, I would like to maintain the fundamental possibility of correction on the basis of scripture – although new insights into scripture would be limited insights as well. And that raises immediately the next question: Which interpretation is the best: that of the past, for example of the church fathers or of the Reformers, or that of the present, our interpretations?

This question is the more urgent for the World Alliance of Reformed Churches, because two-thirds of this "world communion of Reformed churches" consists of young churches from Africa and Asia. Within these churches a similar urge for their own witness of faith *in tempore* and *in loco* may be observed as with the Reformed fathers from the 16th century onwards. The best-known of these new confessions is probably the Belhar confession of 1982, a fierce challenge formulated from the circles of the Nederduitse Gereformeerde Sendingskerk (NGSK) in South Africa against the theology behind the South African policy of apartheid.[13]

With respect to these new confessions Vischer, in his preface to *Reformed Witness Today*, raises a number of hermeneutical questions. He asks, for example,

> How is the relation of the old and the new to be understood? Are the earlier confessions the criterion for judging the new? Or are the old to be read in the light of the new?... How are the differences to be evaluated?[14]

Vischer here raises the question of the criteria for the continuity of a tradition. This question is especially complicated in relation to the Reformed tradition, because within this tradition there has never been *one* church which wished to make its confession the only recognized confession – although many a church cherished, and sometimes still cherishes, this as its most profound wish. Vischer argues, however, that a concrete attempt towards this has never been undertaken. Nevertheless there is certainly for Reformed churches a great, and even growing, need for an exchange of insights on the fundamental issues they face as they confess the faith in their situation. Thus even a legitimate contextual confession such as, for example, the Belhar confession needs a certain exchange both with other contemporary confessions and with the confessions of the past.

The "church-dissolving" element within the Reformation

This great need for exchange is not new within the Reformed tradition. From the very beginning one realized that the church of Christ is greater than one's own church, that it is impossible to *be* church when isolated from other, fellow baptized believers. This awareness of the need for communion with other believers, those elsewhere in the present and in the past, has been enhanced by the admission that the principle of *sola scriptura* contains not only a "church-reforming element", but also a "church-dissolving" element.

I derive the formulations "church-reforming" and "church-dissolving" from one of the greatest thinkers of the Dutch Reformed tradition, Herman Bavinck. In his 1888 rectorial address on the "Catholicity of Christendom and the Church",[15] he argues that an unbridled appeal to scripture also opens the way to a sectarianism in which every heretic has his own (scriptural) "letter of the law". Bavinck rightly puts his finger on the strongly individual character of the Calvinist attitude towards faith, which also leaves its traces in the attitude towards the church.

It is this attitude towards faith in particular which, in the field of the doctrine of the church, has been converted into the striving for the purest church, the *ecclesia purissima*. And it was this very striving which – in spite of all honest intentions – left a trail of destruction in the Reformed churches. It degraded the church to a random group of kindred spirits, while seriously underestimating the role of the church as a mother, to use a expression of Calvin himself.[16] The idea that the church existed long before us, and is *the* instrument of God's loyalty to us throughout the ages, was developed in the Reformed tradition in the theology of the covenant. Unfortunately, however, in the Reformed tradition there has been always an unresolved tension between the doctrine of the covenant and that of the election. Because of this, the doctrine of the covenant could not assume the central place in Reformed ecclesiology which is rightfully its own.[17]

Calvin's preface to the Geneva catechism

As a counter-movement against a certain sectarianism in the Reformed tradition, there have been unmistakably universalizing tendencies as well. A good example of this is Calvin's preface written in

1545 for his own Latin translation of the Geneva catechism of 1542. There he writes,

> We should apply ourselves with all possible means so that the unity of faith, so much recommended by Paul, may again become strong among us. With a view to this goal, the solemn profession of faith *(solennis fidei professio)*, which is part of the common baptism, should especially be applied. It would be desirable that there be a permanent unanimity among all with respect to the doctrine of piety, and also *one* catechism *(unam formam catechismi)* for all churches.

In the continuation of his preface, however, Calvin immediately points out that he is a realist:

> For many different reasons, however, it will always remain so that each church has its own catechism. Therefore, we should not put too much pressure on it, as long as the difference in the way of education does not prevent us from thereby being led towards the one Christ.[18]

For Calvin this piously formulated view of reality is not a stop-gap intended to make a virtue of necessity, as appears from the concrete suggestions he makes for preserving unity in Christ. Thus, first of all, he considers it useful that there are public testimonies *(publica testimonia)* whereby churches separated geographically, but still uniform in doctrine in Christ, mutually acknowledge one another. Calvin points out that for this purpose bishops in former times used to send synodal letters. Certainly now that Christianity is suffering from such an upheaval, he considers it necessary that each one be given this token of holy communion *(sacra communio)*, and that each accept the same from others. In so many words Calvin formulates three criteria for genuine ecumenism: open, public professing; intensive correspondence; and mutual recognition.

The endeavour for a Harmonia Confessionum

Apparently Calvin's ecumenical disposition was known in Europe. Seven years later, in 1552, Thomas Cranmer, the archbishop of Canterbury, approached him with a concrete plan for arriving at a mutual recognition of confessions of faith, and thus perhaps even at a common confession of faith. Calvin was very enthusiastic in his reaction: he would be prepared, he wrote to Cranmer, to cross ten seas for that.[19] But there was not much progress in giving concrete shape to carrying out the plan, as a result of subsequent political developments particularly in Germany and England. In the end the idea of a common confession of faith was abandoned.

In 1581, however, something arose which, in a sense, may yet be considered as an echo of the plan for a common confession. A *Harmonia Confessionum* was drawn up, a collection of Reformed and Lutheran confessional writings which are more or less considered to be in harmony with each other. Later editions of 1612 and 1652 even included the confession of Cyrillus, the patriarch of the Greek church of Constantinople, who was in touch with Reformed persons. An important change in these later editions is also that they opened with the apostolic confession of faith as a common symbol of faith, and concluded with an elaborate paragraph emphasizing the agreement of the content of the confessions of faith with the ecumenical councils and church fathers. In this way there was an attempt to formulate the *consensus catholicus* with the ancient church.[20]

There has never been an edition of a *Harmonia Confessionum* which gained church authority, but the effort towards such a *Harmonia* is, nevertheless, characteristic of a certain spiritual attitude, one which breaks through the strict particularity of one's own national church and expressly looks for continuity with the church of all times and places. It is at least a kind of minimum goal, whereas the maximum goal of one *single* confession of Protestants in Europe has proved to be unattainable.

More than a century later, on the eve of the Enlightenment, we see again some efforts to arrive at a common confession – this time not only between Protestants, but also between Protestants and Roman Catholics. It emerged around the person of Leibnitz; but also this bold plan, brilliantly described with a great feeling for drama by the French historian Paul Hazard in his extraordinary study on *La crise de la conscience européenne*,[21] was doomed to failure.

The Reformed tradition and the World Council of Churches

We may conclude that the Reformed tradition never lost any sense of unity with the church of all ages and centuries. However, whenever Christians put to themselves the question of their common confession of faith there are always two fundamental options: either, in light of the idea "we are not the first", to conform to that cloud of witnesses who went before us; or to listen to the voice of contemporary witnesses of faith around us.[22]

It seems beyond question that when, at the Faith and Order plenary commission meeting in Louvain in 1971, the World Council of Churches started the project towards a "common expression of faith", precedence was given to the second approach. This means: to listen to what is *unanimous* in the midst of the multitude of voices of all those who continue to hope against all odds. At that time, the tenor at Louvain was quite expressly the idea that "the common expression of our faith" can be adequately formulated in only *one* way, namely "by giving account of the hope within us". From the impressive, sometimes even heart-rending, testimonies collected within the framework of this project from many continents, it is clear that a contextual approach towards a common articulation of faith was thought of in the first place.[23] But from this approach it is also clear that it is not at all easy to trace what is "common" among the multitude of witnesses.

That is why within the World Council of Churches a counter-movement soon commenced which, looking back historically, based itself on a so-called "building period" of the church. On the basis of a kind of *principium quinque-saecularis*, for example, the first five centuries of the church are declared to be constitutive for its consequent history in such a way that the formation of the confession during these centuries acquires something of a sacrosanct status.

This approach, however, also raises many complicated questions: for example, that of the exact historical circumstances in which the first creeds were formulated. Were not these creeds, too, products of very specific contexts which cannot simply be universalized? To ask this question is to say, in so many words, that also in refererring to the creeds of the ancient church it is impossible to avoid the question of the mediating role played by the context involved.[24]

Every testimony of faith bears the traces of the time and the place in which that testimony is pronounced. This might be music to Reformed ears, if it were not that this recognition immediately rebounds on their own tradition like a boomerang. For do not Calvinists themselves tend to speak about a "constitutive" period in church history, expressly exempted from the vortex of history, namely the initial period of the Reformation? Do they also not start from a kind of "building" period of the church, namely the 16th century?

Moreover, it will be clear that an explicit approach based on the particularity of every tradition does not facilitate mutual recognition and acknowledgment of one another in world Christianity. Nor do the common witness and the common activity of Christians, in relation to the challenges with which we are confronted by our present-day worldwide society, seem to benefit from an exclusivist contextualization of our expressions of faith.

It might be especially the task of the "Reformed tradition" in world Christianity to cope with this tension between particularity or contextuality on the one hand, and universality or catholicity on the other (and that without completely identifying the latter two concepts).[25] The Reformed tradition has left shameful marks of division of the faith throughout the history of Christianity; that is the bad example of the Reformed tradition. One might, however, also speak of an *illuminating* example. There are not many comparable traditions where the inculturation of the gospel has left such inspiring marks: for more than two decades it is impossible to imagine the WARC without the remarkable voices of, for example, the churches of Korea, Taiwan, India, Indonesia and black South Africa.

During its general council at Seoul, Korea, in 1989 the WARC stated the following about the relation of gospel to culture: "'The gospel' must not be used to promote a 'levelling out' of culture, everything the same everywhere." It is acknowledged that the gospel illuminates every culture, that it holds every culture, as it were, up against the light of the proclamation of Christ. But up to a certain limit it is also acknowledged that every culture illuminates our understanding of the gospel: "Different cultures can perceive in the gospel that which other cultures had failed to perceive."[26]

The Reformed tradition: an interplay of contextual expression and universal truth

My conclusion is, therefore, that the Reformed tradition is preeminently a tradition in which the contextual articulation of faith has acquired a legitimate place – but also in which, nevertheless, the intention of formulating contextually the universal truth in Jesus Christ was upheld continuously and seriously. Especially from the Reformed tradition we can learn that applying an authentic sense of unity does not mean refraining from contextuality, but rather adhering to a kind of contextuality that exceeds its own boundaries in order to proclaim the worldwide dimensions of the gospel.

Just as a contextual interpretation of the gospel does not in itself imply a legitimization of the local situation, likewise it is not, by definition, bound to a specific context. When, for example, an interpretation of the gospel in a particular situation points to injustice or to liberation or to forgiveness, this interpretation is not simply a contextual claim. It may provide an insight to be tested and amended or applied in other contexts as well. The reflection of Bonhoeffer, King, Gandhi and Romero, among others, on their particular situations are instructive examples of the universalizing potentialities of many particular situations. No contextual interpretation, however, can claim to be absolute. Thus the gospel is contextual in that it is inevitably embodied in a particular culture; it is catholic in that it expresses the apostolic faith handed down from generation to generation within the communion of churches of all particular places and ages.[27] May this awareness of our necessarily contextual –

and therefore incomplete – understanding of the gospel be of great help in articulating what unity really is, when local churches are in a uniting process.

NOTES

[1] Cf. for a notable description of the situational character of the Reformed tradition of confession, the Roman Catholic author B. Gassmann, *Ecclesia Reformata. Die Kirche in den Reformierten Bekenntnisschriften*, Freiburg-Basel-Vienna, 1986.

[2] Cf. L. Vischer ed., *Reformed Witness Today: A Collection of Confessions and Statements of Faith Issued by Reformed Churches*, Evangelische Arbeitsstelle Ökumene Schweiz, Veröffentlichung 1, Bern, Evangelische Arbeitsstelle Ökumene Schweiz, 1982, p.7.

[3] Cf. A.P.F. Sell, *A Reformed, Evangelical, Catholic Theology: The Contribution of the World Alliance of Reformed Churches 1875-1982*, Grand Rapids MI, Eerdmans, 1991, pp.74-75.

[4] See "The Notion of 'Hierarchy of Truths': An Ecumenical Interpretation. A Study Document Commissioned and Received by the Joint Working Group", in *Joint Working Group between the Roman Catholic Church and the World Council of Churches, Sixth Report*, Appendix B, Geneva-Rome, WCC Publications, 1990, pp.38-46.

[5] For attempts to trace that "mobility" to a certain degree see among others K. Blei, "The WARC in Bilateral Dialogue", in H.S. Wilson ed., *Bilateral Dialogues*, Studies from the World Alliance of Reformed Churches, 14, Geneva, WARC, 1993, pp.14-15; H.M. Vroom, "On Being 'Reformed' ", in C. Lienemann-Perrin, H.M. Vroom and M. Weinrich eds, *Reformed and Ecumenical. On Being Reformed in Ecumenical Encounters*, Currents of Encounter: Studies on the Contact between Christianity and other Religions, Beliefs, and Cultures, 16, Amsterdam-Atlanta, Rodopi, 2000, pp.153-69; and L. Vischer, "The Reformed Tradition and its Multiple Facets", in J.-J. Bauswein and L. Vischer eds, *The Reformed Family Worldwide: A Survey of Reformed Churches, Theological Schools and International Organizations*, Grand Rapids MI, Eerdmans, 1999, pp.1-33.

[6] Cf. H. Heppe, *Reformed Dogmatics: Set Out and Illustrated from the Sources*, Grand Rapids MI, Eerdmans, 1978, esp. pp.33-41.

[7] Cf. *Seoul 1989: Proceedings of the 22nd General Council of the World Alliance of Reformed Churches, Presbyterian and Congregational, Seoul, Republic of Korea, August 15-26, 1989*, Edmond Perret ed., Geneva, WARC, 1989, p.171.

[8] Cf. L. Vischer, "Witnessing in Unity", in *Mission in Unity: Towards Deeper Communion between Reformed Churches Worldwide,* John Knox Series 8, Grand-Saconnex, Centre international réformé John Knox, 1993, pp.3-14, esp. p.6.

[9] J. Koopmans, *Het oudkerkelijk dogma in de Reformatie, bepaaldelijk bij Calvijn*, Wageningen, Veenman, 1938, p.108; German transl. *Das altkirchliche Dogma in der Reformation*, Beiträge zur evangelischen Theologie, Bd. 22, translated from the Dutch by H. Quistorp, Munich, Kaiser, 1955.

[10] Cf. G. Wenz, "Das Schriftprinzip im gegenwärtigen ökumenischen Dialog zwischen den Reformationskirchen und der römisch-katholischen Kirche. Eine Problemskizze", in H. H. Schmid and J. Mehlhausen eds, *Sola Scriptura. Das reformatorische Schriftprinzip in der säkularen Welt*, Veröffentlichungen der Wissenschaftlichen Gesellschaft für Theologie, Gütersloh, Mohn, 1991, pp.304-16, esp. p.313.

[11] C. Augustijn, *Kerk en Belijdenis,* Cahiers voor de gemeente 7, Kampen, Kok, 1969, p.39.

[12] "Contemporary Questions Concerning the Sola Scriptura", *Reformed World,* 39, 1986, pp.453-73, in particular p.466. The first draft of the paper was drawn up by H.M. Vroom of the Free University of Amsterdam.

[13] For the English text of this confession see, among others, C. Villa-Vicencio ed, *Between Christ and Caesar: Classic and Contemporary Texts on Church and State*, Grand Rapids MI, Eerdmans, 1986, pp.241-43.

[14] Vischer, *Reformed Witness Today*, p.8.

[15] Originally in H. Bavinck, *De Katholiciteit van Christendom en Kerk: rede gehouden bij de overdracht van het rectoraat aan de Theol. School te Kampen op 18 Dec. 1888*, Kampen, Zalsman, 1888; see the reprint of this text prefaced by G. Puchinger: Kampen, Kok, 1968, p. 38: "In the Protestant principle, next to a church-reforming element, there is indeed a church-dissolving element. The one Christian church has fallen apart into countless small churches and sects, of associations and societies."

[16] On the question of "Why do Reformed churches so easily divide?" see Vischer, "Witnessing in Unity", pp.7-10, where he quotes Calvin from *Institutes*, IV, 1.4: "There is no way of entering permanent life other than through being conceived in the womb of this mother; she has to give birth and to feed us with her breasts; she has to sustain and to guard us under her guidance and government until we shall be freed from this flesh and shall be like angels." For the Latin text from the Institutions of 1559 see P. Barth and W. Niesel eds, *Johannis Calvini Opera Selecta*, vol. V, Munich, Kaiser, 1974, p.7. For Calvin's thought on the image of the church as a mother see L. Schümmer, *L'Ecclésiologie de Calvin à la lumière de l'Ecclesia Mater: Son apport aux recherches ecclésiologiques tendant à exprimer l'unité en voie de manifestation*, Zürcher Beiträge zur Reformationsgeschichte, 11, Bern, Peter Lang, 1981.

[17] For the origin of the idea of the covenant in Calvinist theology see D.A. Weir, *The Origins of the Federal Theology in Sixteenth-Century Reformation Thought*, Oxford, Clarendon, and New York, Oxford UP, 1990. On the tensions raised by this theology within Calvinism in relation to the doctrine of election see C. Graafland, *Van Calvijn tot Comrie. Oorsprong en ontwikkeling van de leer van het verbond in het Gereformeerd Protestantisme*, 3 vols, Zoetermeer, Boekencentrum, 1992-1996, and *Van Calvijn tot Barth. Oorsprong en ontwikkeling van de leer der verkiezing in het Gereformeerd Protestantisme*, 's-Gravenhage, Boekencentrum, 1987.

[18] For Calvin's Latin translation see *Corpus Reformatorum*, vol. 34: *Joannis Calvini Opera*, vol. VI, pp.1-146, esp. pp.5-6.

[19] Both Cranmer's letter to Calvin of 20 March 1552 and Calvin's answer, by the end of April or early in May 1552, are to be found in the *Corpus Reformatorum*, vol. 42: *Joannis Calvini Opera*, vol. XIV, p.306 and pp.312-14.

[20] On this cf. H.H. Kuyper, *De Katholiciteit der Gereformeerde Kerken: Afscheidscollege 1 juni 1937*, Kampen, Kok, 1937, pp.18-19. The full title of the first edition of the collection published in 1581 was *Harmonia Confessium Fidei Orthodoxarum et Reformatarum Ecclesiarum, quae in praecipius quibusque Europae Regnis, Nationibus et Provinciis, sacram Evangelii doctrinam pure profitentur*.

[21] P. Hazard, *La crise de la conscience européenne: 1680-1715*, Paris, Boivin, 1935.

[22] On these two possible ways see extensively L. Vischer, "Confessio Fidei in der ökumenischen Diskussion" in G.J. Békés and H. Meyer eds, *Confessio Fidei, International Colloquium Rome, 3-8 November 1980,* Studia Anselmiana, 81 – Sacramentum, 7, Roma, Pontificio Ateneo S. Anselmo, 1982, pp.17-36, esp. pp.17-20. Cf. also L. Vischer, "An Ecumenical Creed?", in *Concilium,* 14, 1978, 8, issue no. 118 on "An Ecumenical Confession of Faith?", pp.95-109.

[23] For the intention of this study project see *Faith and Order Louvain 1971: Study Reports and Documents*, Faith and Order Paper no. 59, WCC, 1971, pp.215,216,239-40. Here one observes with respect to the study: "At this preliminary stage our suggestion is that individual groups reflect on and bring to expression what they understand as the salvation of God, for which they give thanks in worship, and which they are commissioned to proclaim. The task should be approached by groups in various situations, consisting both of members of different churches, and of members of the same confessional families" (p.215). Then under the heading of "Conspectus of studies to be carried out", the project "Common Expression of Faith" is mentioned as the first area for work in the coming years, and is given the subtitle "Giving account of the hope that is in us; cf. 1 Peter 3:15" (p.239). About the purpose of this project it is said: "The study will not aim at the formulation of a creed or confession; it will rather be an effort to give account of our faith today" (p.239). For the result of this study project see the many, often very impressive witnesses of hope from the various continents in the volumes edited by the Taiwanese theologian Choan-Seng Song, *Giving Account of the Hope Today,* Faith and Order Paper no. 81, WCC, 1976;

and *Giving Account of the Hope Together*, Faith and Order Paper no. 86, WCC, 1978; and, further, the reports at the Faith and Order meetings at Accra and Bangalore, *Accra 1974: Uniting in Hope, Reports and Documents from the Meeting of the Faith and Order Commission,* Faith and Order Paper no. 72, WCC, 1975, pp.25-80; and *Bangalore 1978: Sharing in One Hope: Commission on Faith and Order*, Faith and Order Paper no. 92, WCC, 1978, pp.1-11 and pp.51-202.

[24] For that mediating context see e.g. the contributions by A. Heron on "The Historically Conditioned Character of the Apostles' Creed" (pp.20-26) and by Ch. Kannengiesser on "Nicaea 325 in the History of Christendom" (pp.27-35) in *Concilium*, 14, 1978, no. 8, special issue on "An Ecumenical Confession of Faith?". See also M.E. Brinkman, *Progress in Unity? Fifty Years of Theology within the World Council of Churches: 1945-1995*, Louvain Theological and Pastoral Monographs 18, Louvain, Peeters, and Grand Rapids MI, Eerdmans, 1995, pp.61-63.

[25] Universality points to the synchronic aspect of Christianity. Catholicity points at once to the synchronic as well as the diachronic aspect, and moreover points to the content of the Christian message throughout all ages and places, namely to the "being in Christ" of all Christians.

[26] *Seoul 1989*, pp.177-78.

[27] See for a more elaborate version of this interpretation of the relation between particularity and catholicity, M.E. Brinkman, "The Theological Basis for the Local-Universal Debate", in L. J. Koffeman and H. Witte eds, *Of All Times and of All Places: Protestants and Catholics on the Church Local and Universal,* IIMO Research Publication, 56, Zoetermeer, Meinema, 2001, pp.171-85.

The Ghanaian Ministry for London

A Case Study on Unity

FRANCIS AMENU

The main purpose of this case study on unity is to present how the Ghanaian Ministry for London – the sponsored partnership programme between the United Reformed Church (URC) in the United Kingdom, the Presbyterian Church of Ghana, and the Evangelical Presbyterian Church, Ghana – is helping to bring the Ghanaian community in London into a state of unity with the indigenous Christian community, in particular the United Reformed Church in London. This is facilitated by my mandated role as a bridge-builder and reconciler.

The programme started initially as the Ghanaian chaplaincy in the early 1960s, in response to the poor welcome (and indeed racism) faced by Ghanaian students who travelled to Britain for academic purposes. It was, therefore, started with the stated purpose of keeping Ghanaians faithful to Christ and to the church when far from home, and also of providing them with adequate pastoral and practical care. However, the post, which is funded by the URC, has grown over the years from a chaplaincy to Ghanaian students to a position directed towards breaking down barriers between British and Ghanaian Christians. It does this by affirming the role of the ethnic minorities in their membership in British churches, as well as by building bridges of unity and mission within the Ghanaian Christian community itself. So from the very beginning one of the major goals of this ministry has been the reconciliation of these previously divided parties – parties which, even today, continue to grapple with issues of racism, individualism, prejudice, fear and suspicion of the other.

A Ghanaian approach to unity and the nature of the church

With their socio-cultural understanding of the family, Ghanaians often bring the values of the extended family system to bear on their perception of the church as a fellowship of brothers and sisters who belong to the same Father-Mother God. This factor plays a very important role in their seeking membership in churches. Once an individual is genuinely welcomed into a particular church family this prepares the ground for others to follow because they are able to identify, on a relational basis, with members of that fellowship. So the Ghanaian will find it easy to associate with a church in which he or she finds acceptance as a brother or sister. In this process all needlessly divisive factors are, ideally, suppressed. This corporate approach to society, seeing all humanity as the one family of God, is reflected in such communal social structures as the clan, the extended family, and complex networks of social relationships, as well as in the African custom of opening one's door to strangers and showing them acts of generosity and hospitality.

Forging unity between Ghanaian and non-Ghanaian members within the URC

For the purpose of this study it is important to note that the composition of the URC, particularly in London, is both multicultural and multi-ethnic. Apart from the indigenous British members of the URC there are significant proportions of other ethnicities, such as Ghanaians and the Afro-Caribbean members. There are approximately 200 local churches in the London area, with a total membership of about 14,000. At least 2000 of those members are black or Asian, with Ghanaians forming the largest single group within that category. There are a significant number of black or Asian elders in these churches, again with Ghanaians forming the largest group. Ten of the approximately eighty ministers in pastoral charge are black or Asian; four of them, at present, are Ghanaian. Looking beyond the local church context, up to the recent past one would hardly see a black face at district council and provincial synod meetings. But with the sort of encouragement the minority ethnic groups are receiving – and my ministry is part of this process – the pattern is gradually changing. Now central church, synod and district committee members; church-related community workers; elders and both stipendiary and non-stipendiary ministers are all emerging from the fold of ethnic minorities, including Ghanaians. Twenty-five years ago it would have been unthinkable to have ministers from the ethnic minorities in pastoral charge in British churches such as the United Reformed Church. But, thank God, this is now a reality.

A continuing challenge

However, although the barriers of non-acceptance and poor welcome may be falling away, full and productive participation of the ethnic minorities in the life and witness of the United Reformed Church, and other British churches, is still a long way off. It is true that in most (though certainly not all) local URC churches native British are still the majority; yet the proportion of black elders still does not reflect the number of black members found in URC churches, and the native British often dominate the eldership even in churches where they are in the minority. There are also acts of mistrust, racial prejudice and a culture of fear and suspicion, which on careful analysis very often turn out to be based on sheer ignorance and non-exposure to the enduring cultural values of the "other". The Ghanaian Ministry works towards overcoming the ignorance, fear, mistrust and prejudice often found among some native British URC members.

Basic to this is the need to recognize that every ethnic minority immigrant, even if he or she is not a refugee but has freely chosen to come to Britain, may well be a victim of many kinds of loss – loss of the extended family relationship, loss of the status and authority enjoyed in the home society and church, loss of familiar foods, climate and lifestyle. These losses can affect the behavioural patterns of some immigrants. Also most Ghanaian Christians are still closely connected to their home denomination in Ghana which, in turn, has maintained its particular relationship to its "mother" church in the West. This can result in a nostalgia for traditions and liturgical practices not often found in a URC church in London. My ministry is thus geared towards helping the URC members and leadership to understand fully the socio-cultural worldview of the Ghanaian and, where appropriate, other minority ethnic groups within the church and larger community.

My major work in this area, therefore, is to raise the profile of the Ghanaians and thereby give them confidence in their contribution to the life of the church. My presence as visiting preacher in local churches Sunday by Sunday contributes to this, and I make a point of meeting with Ghanaians in the congregation afterwards to hear their stories. I personally make my presence felt in synod and district council and thus encourage Ghanaian membership. The strengthening of their confidence is necessary for building bridges of understanding. I work with the URC's London urban churches group, which also seeks to build confidence for all the ethnic minority members in the London churches. It does this by bringing them together from time to time for support and inspiration through worship and fellowship, and through encouraging them to take leadership roles and to engage in leadership training.

Diverse gifts for the benefit of all

With increased confidence, the Ghanaians are able to offer the URC the blessing of their gifts of hospitality, sense of community, corporate responsibility, and joyful singing and dancing (for example, at the time of the offertory). For without paying the required attention to sensitive issues of this nature, and thereby creating the space and time necessary to do them justice, Ghanaians will rather turn to forming their own churches where they can receive the requisite spiritual, moral, psychological and physical support.

Besides building the confidence of the Ghanaian church members, I am involved in working to increase the understanding of the native British church members, elders and ministers. For example, I am involved in organizing visits to Ghana by white URC ministers who minister to Ghanaians, in order that they can learn more about Ghanaian spirituality and Ghanaian rites of passage.

My personal role at all kinds of church and socio-religious meetings is as an interpreter, enabler, advocate and reconciler. What is needed is for both the native British and the ethnic minority church members to be encouraged to show, in an atmosphere of enduring welcoming and genuine hospitality, mutual respect. This means exhibiting the spirit of tolerance and effectual empathy, and being ready to recognize the potentialities and contributions of the other, in a state of caring love.

This ministry is also helping to make it possible for Ghanaians, the Ghanaian churches, and church leadership in Ghana to know more about the churches in the UK, and about the great ecumenical work of the URC in particular as a church which networks in many mission endeavours with most of the other major denominations. In addition, the work and role of the Ghanaian minister forms the necessary official link between the URC and the other English churches in the UK in which Ghanaians are found, as well as between the Presbyterian and other churches in Ghana. It also serves as the official link between the church and the state; this is seen in the bond between the Ghanaian Ministry on the one hand, and the Ghana High Commission and the various Ghanaian unions and associations (to which most of the church members also belong) on the other, in their various interactions with British society.

Healing divisions within the Ghanaian Christian community

My ministry is also one of providing healing for the Ghanaian Christian community in London at places where there are divisions. The legacy of establishing churches along tribal or ethnic boundaries as practised by the missionary societies is one of the notable contributors to division among Ghanaians. Most Ghanaians normally belong to churches in Ghana before coming to the UK, and once in the UK may wish to continue to identify with Christians belonging to their own denominations. Others respond to ecumenical programmes on the basis of some negative socio-political factors by which they felt victimized when they were in Ghana. Thus they are very suspicious of sharing fellowship – even ecumenically, in the UK – with someone whom they associate in some way with their oppressive situation in Ghana. Those connected with the Pentecostal churches, charismatic churches and other New Religious Movements very often also prefer to work and worship with similar traditions rather than with other Ghanaians. Thus the different church groupings need to be encouraged to work and worship in an ecumenical setting. Ministry is therefore provided through organizing Ghanaian family services every third Sunday of the month, officiating at rites of passage, leading prayer service at Ghanaian association festivals, offering counselling services, and engaging in hospital and home visits.

In being conscious of the above the Ghanaian Ministry is geared towards providing a concrete atmosphere of positive support and cooperation among all the different ethnic groupings, and thereby ensuring the continuation of participatory worship and the mission enterprise. Therefore proper recognition is given to the various tribes; this is clearly seen in the provisions made for especially the major Ghanaian language groups to feature, in addition to the English language, in the monthly Ghanaian family services, the annual joint festival of nine lessons and carols, and the Ghanaian independence and republic day anniversary services. One sees in these events the reconciliation of the tribes and languages and denominations, this serving as a strong witness to the notion of unity. There are encouraging examples of some who come to the monthly services as a result of such joint ecumenical services. So identity *as Ghanaians* provides a way of overcoming church divisions, and a way of witnessing to reconciliation in Christ.

Effectual healing necessitates building upon noticeable strengths, reinforcing existing links, and involving all persons, whoever they may be, through the mutual sharing of, and respect for, others' contributions. Carrying this out is not at all smooth sailing. There are times when some of the gifts brought by some groups – for example the gifts of the smaller choir tradition – may not always find favour with the larger groups.

It is worth mentioning that often some of these activities are done by coordinating the activities of the Ghanaian Ministry with the activities of other Ghanaian ministers and pastors in charge of various denominations, particularly in London. This bridge-building and reconciliatory role provided by the Ghanaian Ministry serves significantly as the hub of integration for the Ghanaian community as found in the various Ghanaian and non-Ghanaian churches, associations, unions, and other socio-political settings.

The focus in providing these services is to help in mitigating the forces of division which hamper healing, through endeavouring to find common grounds in worship and mission. Conscious effort is therefore made to recognize and respect the diversity that abounds within the Ghanaian community itself. Faithful engagement in this is meant to emphasize our common heritage as followers of Christ, and members of the commonwealth of believers in whom the kingdom of God is being realized. The joint sponsorship programme of the Ghanaian Ministry makes it possible for the Evangelical Presbyterian Church, Ghana and the Presbyterian Church of Ghana to meet at least once every four or five years to discuss, to take decisions and to plan the future of the ministry with the United Reformed Church. It is worth mentioning that, over the years, this programme is putting these churches in a situation where there is the possibility of engaging each other in talks about uniting.

Genuine challenges are posed by my own role of "being all things to all people" and the undeniable fact that I come from one particular Ghanaian tradition and one ethnic group. This can sometimes be a very difficult hurdle to clear. That this calls for a need to be welcoming, open, loving, transparent and tolerant cannot be over-emphasized. But this need is accompanied by some level of support: in the areas of enablement and reconciliation, I work in partnership with the URC groups and individuals concerned with racial justice and equal opportunities.

Some reference to majority-minority questions

In emphasizing the idea of finding common ground in Ghanaianness, it is important not to overlook the demands of our calling as participants in the *universal* religion of Christianity. Therefore our understanding is that being able to unite Ghanaians will greatly facilitate the possibility of their being drawn, as a more significant group, into the fold of the church – thus enabling their exposure to the larger Christian community of Britain. It should be emphasized, however, that such typical Ghanaian fellowships must not be seen as exclusive and meant only for Ghanaians. Quite apart from spouses of Ghanaians who may want to join in such fellowships, friends of Ghana, and all others without boundary limitations, are honestly welcome to come and share fellowship. This is already being done by some persons.

The question is bound to be asked whether this may threaten the first area of bridge-building, that with the native British. But finding something a threat is often a sign of one's own desire to be very protective of cherished values, and desirous that one's existing equilibrium or "comfort zone" not be disturbed in any way. First of all, helping the smaller fellowships to grow, and thus paving the way for their positive participation in the greater Christian fellowship, can only establish a stronger unity and ecumenical relationship. As rightly stated by one Ghanaian church leader,

> There is the need to clearly observe the balance between maintaining our ethnic identity and relating to sister churches within the worldwide fellowship of

> Reformed churches. Conscious effort needs to be made concerning how we can live in mutual accountability so that we can sustain one another in unity and legitimate diversity and prevent new issues from becoming causes of division within and between churches of the Reformed family.[1]

It is the responsibility of indigenous churches to care for aliens and sojourners, and to show hospitality to strangers, and on the other hand it is the responsibility of immigrant groups to form some connection and identification with the place and the people of their new residence (cf. Jer. 29:7). Whether through integration of immigrants into existing Reformed churches, or through development of relationships between new immigrant churches and an existing church, both groups must learn to place the affirmation of ethnicity *within* efforts of communication and cooperation.

Concluding reflections

For any human society and institution to thrive, there is the need to establish intimate relationships with others. But this is not possible until the individual or group has achieved a sense of what Erik Erikson, in his *Identity and the Life Cycle*,[2] has called "ego identity". The Ghanaian Christian community in the UK needs first of all to achieve a sense of ego identity, by developing intimate relationships with other Ghanaians with whom they share similar thoughts and cultural values. These are the ones who will provide the needed foundational and enabling environment for strong, mutual emotional attachments and support, as often seen for example at times of death, bereavement and funeral rites.

Ethnic minorities are often lost in the crowds of the city, yet no longer feel a part of their home countries, where they may meet with misunderstanding and suspicion. The Ghanaian Christian is therefore seeking an identity. Ethnic minorities often live with the tension of integration *or* assimilation, in their pursuit to seek greater participation in churches in the UK. Thus the question arises first, whether they must give up all the traditional ethnic values in order to be able to live in "the West", or for that matter specifically in the UK? And second, to be able to practise his or her Christian faith in the UK must a Ghanaian, as a member of an ethnic minority, be regarded as an imitation of a European Christian? Or can they be a person with a concrete identity who has been able to accept and appropriate some aspects of present-day British society, and yet still remain Ghanaian?

I believe that valuing the Ghanaian-ness of the Ghanaian members of local churches is indeed also a way to bridge-building – while ensuring that this does not stop at Ghanaian-ness for its own sake. For the

Ghanaian Christian community to make an effective contribution to the life and witness of the British churches, therefore, one must value the mutual *coming together* of these ethnic minority cells to unite with their British counterparts. With the proper understanding of unity in diversity, one is able to see the essence of the church sharing mutually the various gifts of all the diverse members of the body of Christ for the common good. For our purpose that includes the Ghanaian Ministry teaching and encouraging the Ghanaian community, and other ethnic minority groups, to value native British identity, and to appreciate the gifts which it brings into the fold of the "commonwealth of believers" journeying on the way, as a unified people with a mission to the whole world.

My work as the Ghanaian minister for London has revealed a very interesting fact about how identity can play a vital role in Christian unity. Basically, it involves working from the identifiably known to the unknown – just as Christ told his disciples before his ascension, "But you shall receive power when the Holy Spirit has come upon you; and you shall be my witnesses in Jerusalem and in all Judea and Samaria and to the end of the earth" (Acts 1:8). This is a very important methodology in mission strategy. The fact that I am an Ewe-speaking Ghanaian from Ho in the Volta Region makes it possible for me first of all easily to identify, and work with, the known elements in the Ghanaian community here, and then to move to the unknown. Once the initial stage was established, it was easier to move on to win the trust and confidence of others.

The same can be said of moving from known members of my own denomination to those in the Reformed family, then to the general Christian community including Roman Catholics, the Pentecostal groups, charismatic groups, New Religious Movements and beyond, even to the non-Christian members of the Ghanaian and British communities. The goal of our ministry and mission must not be to create an exclusive Ghanaian church, or British church, or any church associated with only one specific culture, but a church that truly reflects our rich diversity and values the gifts and contribution of all.

NOTES

[1] Sam Prempeh, in his sermon to the Ghanaian community in London, May 2000.
[2] New York and London, W. W. Norton, 1980.

The Impact of Unity

A Case Study

LEO J. KOFFEMAN

In the Netherlands three churches – the Netherlands Reformed Church (NRC), the Reformed Churches in the Netherlands (RCN), and the Evangelical-Lutheran Church in the Kingdom of the Netherlands (ELC) – are striving for full organic unity.[1] The expectation has recently been expressed officially that this goal will be reached in the first months of 2004. In this case study I want therefore to focus on three questions with which we have to cope in our unification process. Each of them refers in some way to the impact of unity, and each of them represents a specific concern from the perspective of one of the three churches involved.

Confessional allegiance

The first question, brought forward once again from within the largest partner in the union process, the NRC, is as follows: To what extent are Reformed Christians in the future United church supposed to owe allegiance to Lutheran confessional documents?

For the more traditional Reformed part of the NRC this is a vital question, indeed. Within the framework of characterizing the confessional stand of the church, article I, paragraph 4, of the new church order lists a number of symbols and confessions:

> The church confesses in communion with the confession of its ancestors as verbalized in the Apostles' Creed, the Nicene Creed and the Athanasian Creed – by which it experiences its unity with the universal Christian church – the original Confession of Augsburg and Luther's Catechism – by which it experiences its unity with the Lutheran tradition – the Heidelberg Catechism, the Genevan Catechism and the Belgic Confession with the Canons of Dort – by which it experiences its unity with the Reformed tradition.[2]

The issue here is that basically "the church" as such, as a whole, is said to "experience its unity" with the Lutheran tradition. The exact translation and interpretation of what is meant here is not easy to determine. I would rather suggest something like this: "The church recognizes its connection with [or allegiance to] the Lutheran tradition" (and the other two traditions mentioned). That is, whoever is part of this church relates somehow to the Lutheran tradition, and thus to the original Confession of Augsburg and to Luther's Catechism.

This kind of statement is theologically possible because of the Leuenberg Agreement,[3] which is mentioned in the second sentence of article I, paragraph 5, of the new church order:

> [Furthermore], with the Leuenberg Agreement the church acknowledges that the Lutheran and Reformed traditions share a common understanding of the gospel.

The genesis of this statement would in itself be an interesting case study. Technically speaking, in this text the new church order does not recognize the Leuenberg Agreement as such (as was the case in earlier drafts). The reference to the Agreement could now be left out, and the sentence would still make sense: the church acknowledges that the Lutheran and Reformed traditions share a common understanding of the gospel. But more traditional Reformed persons have their doubts: Do we *really* share a common understanding of the gospel? The most difficult issue here is the doctrine of predestination, which is the central issue of the Canons of Dort and, for part of the Dutch Reformed tradition, is close to being the very heart of Christian doctrine.

However, in the Lutheran tradition predestination plays hardly any role. Can Reformed Christians, then, be expected to recognize their allegiance to the Lutheran tradition? For some of them this is so vital an issue that they are considering leaving the NRC at the very moment of unification.

In by-law (we say "ordinance") 1, synod has tried to meet this kind of concern. The first article says that "the congregations – i.e. all of them – are connected with the confession of the ancestors", and that "the Reformed congregations recognize their special connection" with the Reformed confessional documents (as do the Lutheran congregations with the Lutheran confessional documents). So there *can* be a special allegiance to specific confessional traditions, although this does not deny our general, and common, allegiance to the traditions which all share jointly.

The next paragraph states that the church as a whole recognizes and respects these special connections of the respective congregations. And finally article I, paragraph 3, adds,

> The congregations recognize and respect the [special] connections of other congregations with regard to the confessional documents, and – in obedience to the word of God – are called to persevere and to grow in a common confessing life of the church.

In addition (according to a proposal that will be before synod in November 2002), the option will be created for future ministers to express, before their ordination, their special connection with one of the confessional traditions.

So far these regulations have not convinced or satisfied those concerned. Here the heart of the question is: What will actually be the impact of unity? Synod recognizes the possibility of a special, positive allegiance to one of the two constitutive traditions in the united church, but it rejects the possibility of an exclusive allegiance to one of them. For those opposed to our union plan, precisely the latter is the only acceptable model of unity. They would not disagree with me if I were to say that, in fact, they do not want full organic unity but rather a federation model of church union.

A minority position

The second question, brought forward once and again from within the smallest partner, the ELC, is this: To what extent are Lutheran Christians in the future United church allowed to maintain a certain independence, e.g. manifest in the power to prevent specific synodical actions?

For the ELC, this is a vital question indeed. Only one percent of the future United church will be Lutherans. They will number about 15,000 out of 2.5 million members, and about 60 out of 2200 congregations. The average size of a Lutheran congregation is about 250 members (to be sure, often in a diaspora situation); the average size of a congregation in the future United church will be about 1150 members. In future general synods only 5 out of about 150 synod members "need" to be Lutherans. There can be more – if the classical assemblies[4] (all of which have overwhelming Reformed majorities) happen to appoint a Lutheran delegate; but that is not very likely to happen. So there will always be the possibility of a fully legitimate majority vote, in spite of a unanimous disagreement on the Lutheran side. In response to this situation, church law experts have used a number of legal instruments to safeguard the Lutheran position. I mention the most important ones.

An essential provision is the fact that apart from its general synod the future United church will also have an Evangelical Lutheran synod, based on direct elections by all Lutheran members of the church. Only in some respects will this Evangelical Lutheran synod have a position similar to that of the 75 classical assemblies. That aspect is not decisive; Lutheran congregations are also part of the classical assembly in their regions. The main mandate of the EL synod is different. This is given in by-law 4, article 18, which lists ten tasks, the first two of which are decisive:[5]

- to take care of the preservation of the Lutheran tradition and its service to the whole church;
- to give guidance to life and work of the EL congregations together and to maintain contact with the EL congregations.

But how is this supposed to function, and to prevent the Reformed majority from simply over-ruling the Lutherans again and again? Here a number of other church order instruments are used. For example, in a whole range of situations classical assemblies can take decisions which have a huge impact on a local congregation: they can change the boundaries of local congregations; they can unite or combine congregations with other congregations, even (in extreme situations) against their own will(!), if a judgment is made that there is no possibility of continuing their independent existence; ministers who perform unsatisfactorily can be removed from ministry; the general synod can appoint – or dismiss – members of seminary boards, and so on. In many such cases the regulations stipulate that "in appropriate cases such decisions cannot be taken without the advice or the cooperation or the consent of the EL synod or its board".

The synod of the present ELC has discussed this kind of provision time and again. More than once these meetings have produced a list of issues where – for the sake of the integrity of Lutheran church life – the rights of the Evangelical Lutheran synod in the future church should be expanded. In November 2002 we will probably see the last round of discussions about such issues. The question is, in which cases do we need to specify the conditions regarding advice, cooperation or consent in such matters?

No doubt the majority of synod want to recognize the need to protect the Lutheran minority through establishing a number of specific rights. But every now and then, we hear tired Reformed people argue, "Don't they trust us [the reformed majority], or what? Of course we will always respect and safeguard the Lutheran tradition, with or without these kinds of provisions." And we read in certain conservative Reformed church newspapers that the orthodox Reformed part of the NRC should be given similar rights – perhaps even including an "orthodox Reformed synod".

Again, the actual impact of unity is the heart of the question. Here the issue of power comes in, and in a massive way. We can deal with theological arguments. We have tremendous expertise in finding church law "solutions". But what about the issue of power?

Diversity

The last question, brought forward once and again from within the third partner, the RCN, is the following: To what extent can diversity be accepted within the church without de facto accepting a non-committed disunity?

The RCN is rooted in a quite uniform tradition. Until the late 1960s all congregations within the church maintained roughly the same practice in terms of doctrine, liturgy, discipline and local church organization. Pivotal was the personal public profession of faith which young people would normally make somewhere around the age of twenty. Only these "professing members" could take responsibility for the baptism of their children; only they could participate in the Lord's supper; only they could vote and be elected as elders or deacons. So-called "baptized members", indicating those who have not (yet) made this public profession of faith, could not. More generally speaking, church assemblies would take all disciplinary measures necessary to maintain orthodoxy – or at least uniformity!

Deep down, some people here still have an intense longing for that kind of clarity in church life. But the draft by-law 4, to be voted on in synod in November 2002, makes legal the space – which has existed in practice for some decades now – for a large diversity in this respect. Here the judgment of the local constituency is decisive. The most explicit arrangement in this regard is to be found in article 6, paragraph 8:

> The [local] church council takes no decision to change procedures in the congregation regarding:
> – baptized members answering the baptismal questions,
> – baptized members being admitted to holy supper,
> – baptized members being given active and passive voting rights,
> – the way elections are organized,
> – the issue of giving a blessing to life partnerships other than marriage... without informing and hearing [reactions from] the members of the congregation.

This simple rule regulates the involvement of the constituency in local church life. It refers to a number of provisions in other by-laws. However, at the same time it provides for the possible existence of at least 32 (mathematically, 2 to the power of 5) different types of congregations: in one congregation, baptized members will have no legal rights at all in the areas covered here; in a neighbouring congregation they will be allowed to participate in the holy supper, but they cannot take responsibility for the baptism of a child; in the next congregation the opposite may be the case, but here – contrary to the first and second example – not only the liturgical celebration of civil marriage is possible, and so on.

Again: 32 options, quite apart from the fact that we will have Protestant (united) congregations, Reformed *(hervormde)* "Re-reformed" *(gereformeerde)* and Lutheran congregations. Formally speaking, this brings the number of options to 128! And please allow me to ignore the fact that the by-laws also distinguish three main types of local church organization, each of which can be configured in different ways.

Quite a few members of the RCN feel uncomfortable with this situation. In historical perspective, you can well imagine this. They sometimes say, "Of course, local church life is the heart of the matter. Freedom has a high value. But what is it that is binding us together nowadays?"

Again, the actual impact of unity is the heart of the question. Is the unity which we in the Netherlands seek more than an organizational framework to bring institutions together? And if so, *why* are we striving for that unity anyway? I would not have welcomed the opportunity of receiving this consultation here in Driebergen if I did not wholeheartedly support the unification process. But the question is vital: What is the impact of unity?

I am looking forward keenly to your reactions to my comments and to our situation here in the Netherlands.

Author's addendum

A few months before the Driebergen consultation in September 2002, a time schedule for the final stage of the unification process had become official. The three synods involved were expected to take provisional decisions on full organic unity in June 2003, and a final vote would be on the agenda on 12 December 2003. It happened in just this way. On that day the three synods took their final decisions and on the evening of 12 December 2003, in a solemn celebration in the historical Dome church in Utrecht, representatives of the three synods signed a declaration on unification (printed following the foreword to this volume). As from 1 May 2004, the Protestant Church in the Netherlands exists as the continuation of the NRC, the RCN and the ELC.

Comments on the section on "confessional allegiance" above

In spite of all attempts to meet the concerns of those opposed to union, "principal objections" continue to exist within the NRC. Writing shortly before May 2004, it is clear that at least a number of local NRC congregations will go to court seeking to be able to leave the church without having to leave church properties behind. Nevertheless, the fact remains that in December 2003 the NRC synod decided in favour of unification by a vote of 51 to 24 (68 percent – and a two-thirds majority was required!).

On the section "a minority position"

Before December 2003 rumours were that if unification failed, it would be due to the ELC synod not finding the required 75 percent majority – a high figure indeed. But after the votes were cast the result was 30 to 6 (83 percent!) in favour of union. Since December, confidence within the ELC only seems to increase.

On the section "diversity"

In the final stage of the process, the issue of diversity (focusing on the option of local congregations accepting liturgical blessings on life partnerships other than marriage) in fact troubled the NRC more than the RCN. In the RCN opposition grew weaker. Still, a few RCN congregations are considering leaving the church, mainly due to changing financial arrangements. In December 2003 the RCN synod voted 66 to 6 in favour of unification (not less than 92 percent – here also a two-thirds majority was required!).

Visible unity certainly has an impact.

NOTES

[1] See Leo J. Koffeman, "The Netherlands, Reformed and Lutheran Churches: Netherlands Reformed Church (NRC); Reformed Churches in the Netherlands (RCN); Evangelical-Lutheran Church in the Kingdom of the Netherlands (ELC)", in Thomas F. Best and union correspondents, "Survey of Church Union Negotiations 1999-2002", *The Ecumenical Review*, 54, 3, July 2002, 385-90.

[2] Translation by Henry De Moor, in *Calvin Theological Journal*, 29, 2, Nov. 1994, pp.507-20; unfortunately the text on the *Samen op Weg* web site *(www.sowkerken.nl)* is of less quality. In both cases the English translation refers to the text as decided on in first reading; the final version of the church order will be published on the website as soon as feasible.

[3] From 1 November 2003 the Leuenberg churches have been known as the "Community of Protestant Churches in Europe" (CPCE).

[4] A "classical assembly" (as the NRC calls it) or "classis" (RCN, plural "clases") is what Presbyterian churches call a "presbytery", i.e. a regional body of representatives of local congregations. We will have 75 classical assemblies with, on average, thirty congregations each.

[5] Another interesting task in our context is the second to last: "to maintain the relationship of the church with the LWF".

A Mission of Unity and a Unity of Mission

Perspectives in the Mission of United and Uniting Churches

JERRY PILLAY

In this paper we shall explore three areas:

- the notion and meaning of mission in United and Uniting churches;
- whether union has actually fostered mission, as often been said before union;
- whether United churches, and those on the way to union, practise mission in a way that actually reflects their commitment to unity.

In responding to the above I will relate to the South African experience and more specifically to the union of the Uniting Presbyterian Church in Southern Africa (UPCSA), which was effected in 1999.[1] I hope that you will be able to bring your own personal experiences into contact and dialogue with the reflections I offer.

The mission of the church

In seeking to understand the mission of United and Uniting churches we shall first undertake a general discussion on the mission of the church. It is not my intention to labour long on the latter since much has already been said about this over the years and, more significantly, by the World Council of Churches (WCC). My intention is to trace the *notion* of mission in United and Uniting churches. I believe this comes generally from the ecumenical church, that is, the churches as they relate to one another and witness and work together.

Attempts to define Christian mission have resulted in prolonged and relentless debates. Even more difficult is the task of determining the aims of mission. If we attempt a more specifically theological synopsis of "mission" as the concept has traditionally been used, we note that it has been paraphrased as (a) propagation of the faith, (b) expansion of the reign of God, (c) conversion of the "heathen", and (d) the founding of new churches.[2] Lesslie Newbigin has narrowed these categories into two terms, described as mission and missions. He states,

> The mission of the church is everything that the church is sent into the world to do: preaching the gospel, healing the sick, caring for the poor, teaching the children, improving international and inter-racial relations, attacking injustice.

> The missions of the church is the concern that in places where there are no Christians there should be Christians. In other words, missions means to plant churches through evangelism.[3]

Newbigin adds that the aim of missions should be the establishment of a new Christian community that is as broad as society, and is true to the national situation. He has in mind here the idea of "Christianization", which is highly questionable today in a world that is characterized by religious pluralism and democracy. Moreover, Christianity has lost its position of privilege. In many parts of the world, even in regions where the church had been established as a powerful factor for more than a millennium, it is today a liability rather than an asset to be a Christian.[4] The encouragement given today to interfaith dialogue and cooperation also brings the goal of mission as Christianization into question.

Jerald D. Gort argues that such a Christian community is characterized by reconciliation and peace, but also by justice.[5] This new redeemed community is then equipped for their mission, their life assignment which is to teach, preach, heal, care for the poor and attack injustice. Karl Barth, however, warns us against the dangers of establishing such an exclusive Christian community.[6] He points out that people's chief concern will then be with the saving of their own souls, or their experiences of grace and salvation; in short, with establishing their personal relationship with God.[7] Barth regards this whole understanding of becoming, and being, a Christian as thoroughly unbiblical and egocentric.[8] What makes someone a Christian is not primarily his or her personal experiences of grace and redemption, but his or her ministry: indeed, the Christian receives forgiveness, justification and sanctification in order to become a servant of God in the world.

Lesslie Newbigin, however, is not unaware of such criticism. His immediate focus with regard to mission seems to be ecclesiocentric, but he points out carefully that this is not the only goal of mission. He states that in the past we have largely limited the goal of missions to the conversion of unbelievers and the planting of churches; and he asserts that this must remain the first objective. The trouble comes, however, when this becomes the sum and substance of our missionary endeavour.[9] He thus indicates that fighting against injustices in the world should also be the task of mission.

Writing in a similar vein the Danish theologian, Johannes Aagaard, states that God works through one extraordinary mission and many ordinary missions.[10] The *extraordinary mission* is the mission of Jesus Christ, the mission of the church as manifested in the sending of Jesus Christ and in the calling of the church to its particular vocation of witnessing to the reign of God. The *ordinary missions*, on the other hand, are the missions of the nations, the missions of all the historical agents which cooperate in the building up of human community.[11] Through all aspects of human history – political, economic, cultural and social – human beings are called, as both communities and individuals, to participate in God's providential care for the world.

Mission is thus not limited to the "mere saving of souls" or the "planting of churches". Hoekendijk criticized the "church-centric" view of mission, pointing out that it does not fully correspond with the biblical view of mission.[12] Such a view of mission, though still prevalent, has lost its relevance in the present century,[13] and this shift can be seen in the emerging views of the church and its mission. In this ecclesiology, the church is seen as essentially missionary in its nature: the church is not the sender but the one sent (1 Pet. 2:9). Its mission (its "being sent") is not secondary to its being; the church *exists* in *being sent* and in *building itself up* for the sake of its mission. Missionary work is not so much the work of the church as simply the church at work.[14] More so, it is the church at work in the world. This missionary dimension evokes intentional – that is, direct – involvement in society; it actually moves beyond the walls of the church, and engages in missionary work such as evangelism[15] and work for justice and peace.

The understanding of the church as sacrament, sign and instrument has led to a new perception of the relationship between the church and the world.[16] Mission is viewed as "God's turning to the world"; this represents a fundamentally new approach to theology.[17] This does not mean that the previous paradigm must be cast aside as utterly worthless. Rather the argument will be that, in light of a fundamentally new situation and precisely so as to remain faithful to the true nature of mission, mission must be understood and undertaken in an imaginatively new manner today. In the words of Pope John XXIII spoken in 1963,

> [In] today's world, the needs made plain in the last fifty years, and a deeper understanding of doctrine have brought us to a new situation... *It is not that the gospel has changed; it is that we have begun to understand it better.*[18]

Mission in the perspective of the kingdom of God

In the light of all this, there is a need today for a new definition of mission which is all-embracing and -encompassing. A new comprehensive approach to mission is called for which has a message for both the whole world and the whole person.[19] Kritzinger points out that mission involves the whole person in her or his total situation in response to the whole gospel.[20] And mission is done in the world: its context is the whole of God's creation. He sees in this three biblical notions which together delineate the essentials of mission. The terms *kerygma* (preaching), *koinonia* (fellowship) and *diakonia* (service), in combination, describe the main aspects of the witness (*martyria*) of the kingdom.[21]

What then is mission today? Emilio Castro answers this question succinctly. He states that God's mission, and our mission, is to bring in the kingdom;[22] and the goal of the kingdom is life in its fullness. Hence the kingdom has to do with the welfare of the whole person, not excluding the social, political and economical aspects of life. Since God is interested in the life of the whole person, so must we be also if we are to take our responsibilities of mission seriously. J. Verkuyl supports this view by stating that in both the Old and New Testaments, God by his words and deeds claims that he is intent on bringing the kingdom of God to expression, and restoring his liberating domain of authority. Hence Verkuyl states that the ultimate goal of the *missio Dei* is the kingdom of God.[23] From the countless biblical images and symbols which describe God's intentions, he selects this one as the clearest expression of God and his purpose.[24]

We therefore select the kingdom of God as the central theme through which to understand mission.[25] It would be difficult to find a more inspiring biblical theme as we face the challenges of the contemporary situation. This does not mean, however, that our choice is a matter of convenience. The 1973 Bangkok assembly of the WCC's Commission on World Mission and Evangelism supports our view in the following statement:

> The selection of the symbol of the kingdom of God is not an arbitrary one. Firstly, because it is the central concern of Jesus Christ himself. Secondly, because we believe that it responds to the inspiration of the Holy Spirit that is calling our attention once again to that ongoing memory of the kingdom, to provide the intellectual and inspirational categories that will help the church in its missionary obedience today.[26]

Kritzinger also selects the theme of the kingdom of God in his definition of Christian mission:

> We understand Christian mission to be a wide and inclusive complex of activities aimed at the realization of the reign of God in history. It includes evangelism but is at the same time much wider than that. Perhaps one could say that mission is the "cutting edge" of the Christian movement – that activist streak in the church's life that refuses to accept the world as it is and keeps on trying to change it, prodding it on towards God's final reign of justice and peace.[27]

By defining mission as the establishing of the kingdom of God we are attempting to give a broad definition to mission. We are stating categorically that God's concern is with the whole world and with all humanity, stating with W. Pannenberg that all history is God's history and whatever happens in the world today is also of special concern to God.[28] The Tambaram conference (1938) pointed out that "the kingdom of God is within history and yet beyond history".[29] Whilst we accept the latter, we must nevertheless reiterate the fact that the kingdom is to be understood in present reality, as we work towards the liberation and humanization of the poor and the oppressed.

Unlike Lesslie Newbigin or Johannes Aagaard, we do not see a dichotomy between mission and missions, or between extraordinary and ordinary missions. The one singular mission is the kingdom of God which rules in justice and righteousness. And to this end the ecumenical movement has shown us that the aim of mission includes humanization.

Mission in the United and Uniting churches

This ecumenical perspective on mission is usually embraced by United and Uniting churches. There is a focus beyond the church which relates to the kingdom of God; and it is this imperative that drives these churches into unity. As they join forces they seek to address the problems in the world. This is reflected, for example, in the vision and mission statement adopted by the Church Unity Commission (CUC, in South Africa) in June 2000. The CUC is committed to:

- seek agreement on the ministry of oversight which will make possible the full reconciliation of our ministries and a relationship of full communion;
- hold the churches to their commitment "to work together for the spread of the gospel, for justice, peace and freedom, and the spiritual and material wellbeing of all people; to seek to become a fellowship in Christ which is not divided by tradition, nation, culture, class and colour; to pursue means whereby, under the guidance of the Holy Spirit, our churches in each place may act together in worship, witness and service";
- encourage and facilitate the ministry of reconciliation across the divisions of tradition, nation, culture, class, gender and colour both within and between our churches;
- invite other churches to share with us in the quest for fuller Christian unity;
- involve individual members of our churches in the realization of these aims.[30]

This statement, however, speaks not only about "turning to the world" in mission but also about *uniting* the church so that it may more effectively fulfill its mission in the world. This view on mission can also be seen in the statement issued by the Presbyterian Church of Southern Africa

(PCSA) and the Reformed Presbyterian Church in Southern Africa (RPCSA) as to why they should unite:[31]

- Because a united church is a valid witness to the power of reconciliation in a divided society.
- Because the fullness of Christian truth and worship between the two churches can only be truly expressed in unity.
- Because the church is truly the church when it ignores external factors and denominational labels.
- Because a negative social-political situation has been overcome.
- Because obedience to the gospel demands it.

It can be seen from the above that United and Uniting churches have their mission directed in two ways: firstly to the world, to impact it with the love of Christ, and secondly to work towards the oneness of the church. It is in the latter aspect that they differ from most other churches. These two aspects are related to the one mission of the church: the kingdom of God. Edinburgh 1910 suggested, without spelling it out, that authentic unity could not be had without authentic mission, without an open window towards the world. A WCC meeting in Switzerland recognized that it was inconceivable to divorce the obligation of the church to take the gospel to the whole world from its obligation to draw all Christ's people together; both were viewed as essential to the being of the church and the fulfilment of its function as the body of Christ.[32] Listening to God's word and listening to each other belong together, however; and we can have the first if we are also prepared to have the second.

United and Uniting churches offer a more directed focus to the mission of the church. What are some aspects of this focus on the church's mission? Firstly, it acknowledges that it is the mission of the church to shape a new identity for society. The quest for a new identity is part of a serious effort to discover new values. The South African society has been divided by apartheid; in such a context, a United church consisting of people of different colour and culture presents itself as a witness to healing and reconciliation. Mission thus becomes very contextual.

Secondly, United and Uniting churches embrace a holistic view of mission. The biblical focus of this view on the kingdom of God draws its attention not only to the unity of the church, but also to addressing injustices in the world. Its focus is not limited to the "mere saving of souls" or to "church planting". In this sense it can also offer a collective and strengthened prophetic voice and role in society.

Thirdly, this view of mission promotes values which in turn engender a deep sense of a shared life, a sense of community. The moral imperative confronting the church in promoting new values is to bring people into an authentic relationship with God and with one another, to nurture a community that "breaks bread together" in the African sense of the term. For when bread is shared in our communities it is a symbolism which expresses shared life in all its dimensions. Therefore one of the challenges confronting the church is to be a radically inclusive community revisiting the New Testament idea of *koinonia* as a model for shared existence. Such shared existence is also realized in the sharing of human and material resources.

Fourthly, in South Africa United and Uniting churches, by virtue of their very existence, help in the building of a new nation; and in helping to build the new nation we will also learn how to express our unity in Christ.

Fifthly, such churches are visible as a force for unity and change. By its ecumenical commitment such a church demonstrates the possibility of bringing together people and faith structures which are *diverse* and which point the way to a common commitment.

And sixthly and finally, such a view stands as a visible call to other denominations to heed Jesus' call that "they may all be one". Whilst the above points are not necessarily unique to United and Uniting churches they are, however, found in these churches in a more focused and concentrated form.

Does unity foster mission?

Usually whenever churches seek to unite it is because they believe that it will enhance the mission of the church. However, their attempts at making the union work become themselves a time-consuming "mission". The end result is that they lose sight of the significance of union for their mission to the world. For example, in his report to the CUC member churches in May 2002, CUC general secretary Donald Cragg stated,

> Twenty years later we still have a long way to go. In matters of faith and order we have made progress: we now accept each other's members on transfer without reconfirmation; we accept each other's ordained ministers and permit them to exercise a preaching, teaching, pastoral and sacramental ministry within each of our churches; and we are seeking agreement on the ministry of oversight. [But] partnership in mission is less evident.[33]

We have experienced this also in the UPCSA. In the three years since our union in 1999 we have been focusing on getting the union working. Now that in itself is not a wrong focus. If we are to present a united witness to the world it is of course imperative that we first get our own house in order. However, this cannot, and must not, be the sum total of our church's mission: if this is the case, then we have lost the purpose of union. The problem is that we often lose the purpose as we concentrate on the problems faced in making the union work. Unfortunately, in the process of making union work our focus changes from mission to maintenance. The situation in the UPCSA is also "exhausted" by the lack of energy and resources. We are stalled in our mission by the various methods, practices, styles and even cultural approaches to a range of things things. Reflecting on the UPCSA union, I can point to some of the reasons which are preventing unity in mission:

1) power and personalities: people with influence can either encourage or discourage the union;
2) preservation of certain things from the past: for example, the women's and men's organizations cannot reach consensus on issues of the uniform to be worn;
3) provisions and sustenance of the clergy, that is through pensions, stipends and medical aid;
4) practises and procedures – cases of divorce, assessments, the use of the church manual, and so on;
5) politics – a politically divided church is sensitive to being "politically correct", sometimes at the expense of genuine Christian spirituality.

The question is: Who ought to be the beneficiaries of union? Is it the partner churches? Is it the new denomination? Is it individuals (the clergy)? Often the focus is on these things. For example the former RPCSA is concerned that, within the new church, it is being "swallowed up" by the former PCSA (which was much larger); while members of the former PCSA are nostalgic for their "old" church. The clergy are afraid about provisions for such matters as pensions, medical aid and other pragmatic concerns. While these may be very necessary things, they are not the mission of the church. They are not focused on kingdom ideals, yet we seek to give them value beyond their level of deserving. This poses the question yet again: Who should be the real beneficiaries of union?

The answer to this question is not difficult to find. Jesus' prayer in John 17 sheds light on this question. The real beneficiary should be God: "It is to the Father's glory that we be one." It is in response to this that Moltmann states: "The church's final word is not 'church' but the glory of the Father and the Son in the Spirit of liberty."[34]

Another beneficiary should be the world: "May they be brought to complete unity to let the world know that you sent me and have loved them even as you have loved me" (cf. John 17:23). We gather from this that mission is the comprehensive term for all the conceivable ways in which people may cooperate with God in respect of this world. Barth puts it more clearly: "The church is the community for the world." The church exists not for itself but for its Lord and for others, in the sense that its mission is to be the visible presence of God's love in a hurting and sin-sick world. Mission is summed up in the church's identity: Who are we, and for what are we here?

I have a little reservation about putting our themes for this consultation – unity, mission and identity – in that order, if that means putting them on different levels of significance.[35] For me they are all interconnected and they all have equal importance. But if we had to place them in order of importance, I would put identity first. For me that's the problem with the church: it does not know whose it is, and what it is called to be. Our identity is in Christ. Perhaps we are too focused on what we are supposed to *do* rather than on what we are called to *be*. We are called to be a unity. Our unity is centred on what Christ has called us to be, for him, in the world. The church, then, is challenged not so much to provide a unity but to *be* a unity in a world divided by colour, creed, race, culture and other factors. It does this as it seeks to be more Christ-like; and when it seeks this, it lives not in competition but in contradiction to the world and to worldly values. How the church needs to learn this today!

The apostle Paul is expressive of this in Ephesians 4:1-16. Drawing from what has been said in the previous three chapters, Ephesians 4 shows the church as the recipient of God's love and grace, and thus called to live as such in the world. But how does the church become a "grace extender"? The chapter provides four answers to this question:

1. It proclaims Christ: Paul sees this as his task, even as he describes himself as "a prisoner for the Lord" (Eph. 4:1).
2. The passage describes the way we do mission: "Be completely humble and gentle; be patient, bearing with one another in love" (4:2).
3. The text exhorts: "Make every effort to keep the unity of the Spirit…" (4:3). The way we do that is to fellowship with the Spirit; and only when we live in such full submission will we experience "a demonstration of the Spirit and of power" (1 Cor. 2:4, the theme of the Driebergen consultation).
4. The text urges members of the body to use their grace-gifts to God's glory (Eph. 4:11-16). They do this so that "the body may be built up until we all reach unity in the faith and in the knowledge of the Son of God..." (4:12-13).

United and Uniting churches, it seems, have failed to foster mission because they have tended to focus on one aspect of their mission – namely, a mission of unity. These churches need to return to their source, to appreciate fully and to implement their original focus on the kingdom ideals. Our problem is that while we tend to think kingdom, we often act church. The result is that we become more ecclesiocentric (wanting to protect our vested interests in the church), rather than being kingdom oriented (praying that God's will, and not ours, be done). As United and Uniting churches, we have so much more to offer towards effective Christian mission: (1) we embrace great diversity and seek human community; (2) we have combined resources; (3) we offer a united witness in a divided world; (4) we can show that union works and that the biblical call for church unity is obtainable; (5) we can encourage other churches to seek union; and (6) we can offer a witness to people of other faiths, who usually question the fragmentation of denominationalism. But the question is: Are we succeeding in *using* our strengths?

It is my claim that we are not, because we are failing to be a united witness in the world (we will come to this in the next section). We need to come back to a *theologia crucis*, a theology of the cross of Christ. We need to learn afresh what it means to die to self so that Christ may live. Only when we seek that life as a church will we have true unity in mission; and only then can we have real church unity. Somehow, using all our clever methods, we continue to define and ensure the outcome of our endeavours. But only through the pain of letting go can there be resurrection.

Mission practice

In the days of apartheid in South Africa, churches were committed to working together and they found their unity in the struggle. However, in the last few years there seems to be a growing lack of ecumenical enthusiasm and a growing spirit of denominationalism. John de Gruchy explains this ecumenical apathy:

> There have been setbacks and disappointments, and matters affecting faith and order have clearly not been a priority on the ecumenical church's agenda as we have struggled against apartheid. The truth is that, both in South Africa and universally, the concerns of ecumenical social ethics and those of faith, order and church unity, have often been kept in separate compartments, as though they had little to do with each other.[36]

De Gruchy states that our unity was based on a common social praxis without paying much attention to the theological and confessional issues which divide us. The result is that we have failed to produce leaders with ecumenical vision and commitment. This is part of the reason why we have a resurgence of denominationalism.

The interest in South Africa on the part of foreign partners in mission also seems to have dwindled since the demise of apartheid. They have turned their interest to other parts of the world, where they may once again engage social praxis. They have not continued in the quest for church unity. Does this indicate that their interest is in social praxis, or in the unity of the church? Christian world communions would need to look seriously afresh at their basis of operation. Are we fostering a wedge between the unity of the church and social ministries?

For example, in South Africa the South African Council of Churches (SACC) seems to continue its activist mentality, instead of becoming truly a council of churches. The CUC, it seems to me, sees itself as an arm of the SACC. Whilst its task is to unite churches (organically and communionally, that is), it leaves to the SACC the task of uniting churches in mission. So we have separated unity and mission as if they are two different things. But that is how we function as churches in South Africa: whilst we come together to talk unity, we also return to our quest to preserve our denominational identity and mission. We seek to compete with one another in doing the same things.

For example, we tackle HIV/AIDS denominationally instead of pooling our resources to address the crisis; and we embark on development and poverty alleviation programmes independently, when we could do so much more together. Churches need, at least for a start, what I would call "limited structural" unity if the church is to succeed in its unity in mission. As an example, the CUC should attempt to start a missions department embracing the work of its partner churches.

Even regionally the council of churches seem to be struggling to survive. The interest in ecumenical mission has no doubt dwindled. However, in local communities it seems to be flourishing: ministers' fraternals and local congregations work together to address problems within their communities, and they express a greater desire to work together than churches on the national level. We are thus seeing an increase in local church unity, as members of congregations tend to transcend denominational barriers and focus on human need and Christian witness. If church unity is to be fostered, it is on this contextual level that we will need to put in our energy and resources.

One of the criticisms usually laid against union is that the "grassroots" are often left out of the process, which takes place on a national and international level. The end result is that while union takes place on the national levels of the church, it does not necessarily do so "on the ground"; hence one has a union which works in theory, but not in actual practice. For example, in the UPCSA most of our congregations remain essentially unchanged – and in some cases unaffected – by the union.

Mission usually takes place at the local level; therefore church unity should also begin there if it is to be more effective. Hence international, national and regional structures and organizations should mobilize, empower and enable local church communities for more effective mission and church unity. In order to succeed in the latter area, our mission should be not church but Christ. The truth is that Christ does not belong to us. We are the ones who belong to Christ. Our task is collectively and correctly to read the signs of the times and faithfully proclaim, in word and deed, that God reigns supreme over our world.

Conclusion

Eric Wolf once said that freedom is a process that is forever unfinished. Perhaps the same can be said about the mission of unity and the unity of mission – it remains with us until our Lord returns. But in the meantime let us remain faithful and committed to the prayer of Jesus: "Father, may they be one" (John 17:21). A united Christian witness is bound to help create a better world. Hence we should continue in preserving the goal of Christian unity, and persisting in our search for it, in the churches today.

NOTES

[1] The Uniting Presbyterian Church in Southern Africa (UPCSA) was established in 1999, through the fusion of the Reformed Presbyterian Church in Southern Africa (RPCSA) and the Presbyterian Church in Southern Africa (PCSA).

[2] K. Muller, *Mission Theology: An Introduction*, Nettetal, Steyler, 1987, pp.31-34.

[3] Paul G. Schrotenboer, "Rethinking Missions – in Kingdom Perspective", in *International Reformed Bulletin*, 15, 48, 1972, p.6. See also Lesslie Newbigin, "Mission and Missions", in *Christianity Today*, 4, 22, 1 Aug. 1960, p.23.

[4] In the course of this century the missionary enterprise and the missionary idea have undergone some profound modifications. These came about partly as a response to the recognition of the fact that the church is indeed not only the recipient of God's merciful grace but sometimes also of his wrath. We have seen this in the apartheid church in South Africa.

[5] Jerald D. Gort, "Melbourne 1980: A Missiological Interpretation", in *International Review of Mission*, LXIX, 276-77, Oct. 1980-Jan. 1981, p.568.

[6] D.J. Bosch, "Evangelism and Social Transformation", in *Theologia Evangelica*, XVI, 2, June 1983, p.50.

[7] Barth develops his ecclesiology in three phases. His reflections on soteriology as *justification* are followed by a treatment of "The Holy Spirit and the *Gathering* of the Christian Community". His exposition on soteriology as *sanctification* leads to a discourse on "The Holy Spirit and the *Upbuilding* of the Christian Community". And his discussion of soteriology as *vocation* is followed by a treatise on " The Holy Spirit and the *Sending* of the Christian Community". See David Bosch, *Transforming Mission: Paradigm Shifts in Theology of Mission*, Maryknoll NY, Orbis, 1999, p.373.

[8] Bosch, "Evangelism and Social Transformation", p.51.

[9] Schrotenboer, "Rethinking Missions", p.7.

[10] Emilio Castro, *Freedom in Mission*, WCC, 1985, p.67.

[11] *Ibid.*, pp.68-69.

[12] J.C. Hoekendkjk, "The Church in Missionary Thinking", in *International Review of Missions*, XLI, 163, 1952, p.332.

[13] Even the Pentecostal and charismatic churches in South Africa are showing a greater interest in community work, for example through soup kitchens, skills training, and in other areas.

[14] T.F. Stransky, "Evangelisation, Missions, and Social Action: A Roman Catholic Perspective", in *Review and Expositor,* 79, 1982, pp.343-51.

[15] Even the concept of "evangelism" has a plethora of definitions. See Bosch, *Transforming Mission*, pp.409-20. Our understanding of evangelism involves a broader definition than "merely saving souls" (that is, conversion).

[16] This is contained in the emerging ecumenical paradigm of mission.

[17] L. Hoedemaker, "Het volk Gods en de einden der aarde", in *Oecumenische inleiding in de Missiologie: Teksten en konteksten van het wereldchristendom*, A. Camps, L.A. Hoedemaker, and M.R. Spindler eds, F.J. Verstraelen general editor, Kampen, Kok, 1988, pp. 167-80.

[18] Quoted in G. Gutiérrez, *A Theology of Liberation*, Maryknoll NY, Orbis, 1988, p. xiv.

[19] J.C. Hoekendijk, "The Call to Evangelism", in *International Review of Missions*, XXXIX, 154, April 1950, p.170.

[20] J. J. Kritzinger, *The South African Context for Mission*, Cape Town, Lux Verbi, 1988, p.34.

[21] *Ibid*. We can also add to these a fourth aspect, namely *leiturgia* (worship).

[22] Castro, *Freedom in Mission,* pp.56-60.

[23] J. Verkuyl, *Contemporary Missiology*, Grand Rapids MI, Eerdmans, 1978, p.203.

[24] *Ibid*., p.200.

[25] The term "kingdom of God" is a problematic one. It is feudal, both as a reference point and as an image of relationships that are hierarchical and irrevocably customary. The term is thus anachronistic to notions of democratization, *even* in considering claims about God (that is, the metaphorical base for our language of God). The term is also patriarchal. However in this paper I shall continue to use the term, as an appeal to tradition, for the following reasons: (1) it is biblically based; (2) it is used widely in theological circles; (3) it is a key concept which encourages a Christian involvement in the transformation of the world; and (4) it is commonly used and accepted by local churches. However, in order to maintain my sensitivity to issues of democracy and gender, I shall use the term in inverted commas.

[26] Cf. *Bangkok Assembly 1973. Minutes and Report of the Assembly of the Commission on World Mission and Evangelism of the World Council of Churches, 31 December 1972 and 9-12 January 1973*, WCC, 1973.

[27] Nico Botha, Klippies Kritzinger and Tinyiko Maluleke, "Crucial Issues for Christian Mission – A Missiological Analysis of Contemporary South Africa", in *International Review of Mission,* 83, 328, Jan. 1994, p.21.

[28] Wolfhart Pannenberg, *Revelation as History*, London, Sheed & Ward, 1969, pp.125-30.

[29] See *International Review of Mission*, LXXII, 288, Oct. 1983, p.525.

[30] See Donald Cragg, "Church Unity Commission (CUC)...", in Thomas F. Best and Union Correspondents, "Survey of Church Union Negotiations 1999-2002", Faith and Order Paper no. 192, *The Ecumenical Review*, 54, 3, July 2002, pp.373-78.

[31] See *Presbyterian Church of Southern Africa: Papers for General Assembly 1997*, pp.137-38.

[32] For more on this see Bosch, *Transforming Mission*, pp.376-78.

[33] Available from Donald Cragg, P.O. Box 2651, Pinegowrie, 2123, South Africa.

[34] J. Moltmann, *The Church in the Power of the Spirit: A Contribution to Messianic Ecclesiology*, London, SCM Press, 1977, p.19.

[35] They were placed in this order at the consultation in Driebergen.

[36] J.W. de Gruchy, "Becoming the Ecumenical Church", in *Being the Church in South Africa Today*, B. Pityana and Charles Villa-Vicencio eds, Johannesburg, South African Council of Churches, 1995, pp.12-24.

A Case Study in Mission

The United Church in Jamaica and the Cayman Islands

NORBERT D. STEPHENS

The formation of the United Church in Jamaica and the Cayman Islands in 1965, and its further re-formation in 1992, brought together the ministry and mission heritages of three Reformed denominations: the Congregational Union of Jamaica, the Presbyterian Church of Jamaica and the Disciples of Christ. The missional identities of these churches were shaped within a dehumanizing environment controlled by European political and economic systems of colonialism and slavery. This formation is further enhanced by the fact that the United Church spans two nations, Jamaica and the Cayman Islands.

This paper seeks to identify the significant mileposts along the continuing journey of the United Church towards an understanding of its ethos and the practice of its mission.

The missionary legacy

An analysis of the United Church in Jamaica and the Cayman Islands must begin with its origins and the impact of the missionary legacy in shaping its identity. It is acknowledged that many positive things are to be identified as a consequence of this era of missionary enterprise, especially in the areas of the religious, educational and economic development of the people. But it is also clear that the teething pains of the first twenty years after the union in 1965 were directly influenced by the colonial culture. The value system and assumptions through which the Christian message was communicated gave birth to ways of thinking, worshipping, structuring and operating that were more attuned to a past European missionary era than to the present contextual realities. The critical challenge of this legacy was, and continues to be, how to journey from a Euro-cultured church to one which is able to minister effectively to, and to enable, a black post-slavery people.

As a result we have had to ask ourselves some serious questions in four critical areas of the church's life and witness:

1) gospel and culture: how to understand and share the gospel in culturally relevant ways;

2) worship and fellowship: how to organize the life of the congregations in culturally relevant ways;
3) mission and witness: how to restructure its identity as an organization that "exists for the salvation of others";
4) stewardship of resources: how to maximize the resources of people, property, finance and faith for the church's ministry and mission.

First union

The formation of the union in 1965 and 1992 was strongly motivated by the view of leaders who felt that the new church would be stronger being united than remaining separate as struggling denominations. Although this was true up to a point, the early experience of the union revealed that being changed into a united church was not the same thing as being renewed for mission engagement. The dysfunctional features which had retarded the development of the Presbyterian, Congregational and Disciples of Christ denominations continued to affect the "new church" following the union. The ecclesial seeds that determined the mode, pattern and practice of ministry were more powerful than the seeds for change and renewal. The overall development of the church raised serious questions about its spirituality, style and structure, as seen in the following phenomena:

- a continuing lack of membership growth within an ever-increasing population;
- an ever-increasing growth in the number of small congregations with less than fifty members;
- a growing sense of distance between the local congregations and the synodical office;
- a growing sense of distance between the local congregations and the area council office;
- a growing crisis in financing the church's development, with costs rising faster than the level of giving;
- a growing lack of confidence in the conciliar and committee system, which is perceived to stifle personal leadership and weakens the respect for authority and discipline within the church.

Driven by the prevailing challenges of the time, those who provided leadership had a strong sense of call to bear witness to the unity of the church

Restructuring for renewal

Ethos

Although attempts were made in the mid-1970s to renew the church, the most far-reaching efforts came in 1985. The synod then embarked on a journey to design, develop and implement, in a systematic way, a strategy for renewing and equipping its understanding and practice of ministry. The synod document "Equipping the Church for Ministry and Mission" analyzed the purpose and calling of the United Church, as it existed at that time. It assessed the ways in that the church had – or had not – lived up to its missional identity and purpose. A fourfold plan of action emerged that defined the church's priorities in mission as:

- equipping the church for ministry and mission;
- examining the central administration of the synod;
- funding the church's ministry and mission priorities;
- developing a vision and strategy for spiritual and numerical growth.

This new thrust of the church led it to reformulate its self-understanding. In its mission statement, new emphasis was placed on being a church *for others*. The United Church was convinced that within the context of the liberal/conservative divide, it was not necessary to choose one "side" or the other but to make judgments based on the specific context and climate, while at the same time remain faithful to its history. It felt the need to affirm the strong intellectual competence of its leadership, but wanted equally to respond to its evangelical call. The United Church was known as a socially active church, but felt that its ethos should also embrace a dynamic tension with its sense of call to evangelism. People, rather than funds or assets, were declared to be the most important resource of the church and the ordinary people in the pews were seen as the real agents of the church's ministry and mission. As the church explored its new mission identity, it began to put in place the following changes that would help it realize its potential:

- redefining the ethos of the church through a thorough re-examination of those issues that gave it its unique character;
- renewed emphasis on the social services;
- effective stewarding of its resources;
- developing an integrated personnel development programme for the equipping of lay leaders and some of its clergy.

All the research data on the United Church confirm that the most important challenge facing it continues to be the ineffective mission and ministry development of the local congregations. Most congregations are unclear what they are called to be and to do. Yet if they are to mediate life to others, then it is vital for congregations to give concrete expression to their missionary calling by demonstrating that they can offer an authentic witness to counter alienation and division within the church and the society.

Structures

In order to implement this vision, the synod reorganized its administrative structures. It also put in place a team to restructure the church's finances, so that it would be better equipped to address the needs of its ministry and mission. A ministry trust fund was established. Congregations were challenged to become strategic partners through increased assessment (expected giving), and a systematic plan was adopted to develop the church's property. A number of areas of concern have been addressed in order to maximize our resources. These include the formation of CODAS, a structure for coordination of outreach and development programmes, and the recent appointment of a deputy general secretary located in the Grand Cayman, who is responsible for finance and programmes and is accountable to the synod through the office of the general secretary.

Ministerial formation

The establishment of the Institute for Theological and Leadership Development (ITLD) in 1989 constituted a paradigm shift in the church's approach to ministerial formation. Whilst affirming the role of the traditional residential university-based model, it has recognized the need for a complementary community/congregational based model which would heighten the formation of those seeking to serve and equip the local congregation in ministry and mission. The student population of this degree-granting institution has grown by over 400 percent over the last five years, and continues to be innovative in terms of its model and the delivery of its service. The ITLD is able to celebrate some six hundred students in Jamaica and Grand Cayman who are learning to be learners.

Community leadership

The Mel Natan Institute serves a politically tribalized area and has delivered a variety of ministries aimed at development at all levels – personal, social, economic. The innovation of a preparatory school in an inner-city community, which contradicts assumptions about such communities and highlights the principle of providing quality opportunity for all, is a lesson being appropriated at the moment.

In conjunction with the ITLD's pastoral counselling programme, and in partnership with the government, a ministry focused on the rehabilitation of prisoners is being offered through an established centre.

A working group was formed by the synod's administration in May 1998 to reflect upon a document from the Council for World Mission. The group identified the following positive developments which the church has achieved during its renewal process:[1]

- In all five area councils, personnel development centres were set up through which training courses for a variety lay and ordained groups have taken place. Each centre had a coordinator and a youth minister to develop and coordinate training and youth programmes. Rethinking mission as the responsibility – and privilege – of *every* Christian has been an integral part of all training courses.
- Through the ITLD some sixty pastoral ministers, youth ministers and community workers have been trained within a congregational setting. Most graduates are now working within the United Church, several with quite amazing results in terms of church growth and community outreach.
- A series of liturgy and music events (days, camps, and exchanges of persons and experience) have been held to develop contextually relevant liturgies and liturgical elements such as prayers, litanies, creeds and songs. In recent years, intergenerational music camps have trained potential church musicians in keyboard, drums and other instruments.
- A structure (CODAS) was set up, as noted above, to coordinate the various outreach and development projects of the church, in order to avoid overlap and maximize the effectiveness of programmes and personnel.
- Over the years, the reorganized synodical committees seem to have ensured greater streamlining of training and equipping, mission action and property development. Objectives for all committees have been set systematically, and evaluated in consultation with the newly established central planning committee.
- By 1990 the ministry and mission trust fund became operative. The interest accrued by the fund has been used towards training and equipping for ministry, mission and service.

An honest look in the mirror

The renewal process has helped us look honestly at ourselves as a church. Happily we have found that there is much to celebrate about the United Church in Jamaica and the Cayman Islands:

- Since 1994 we have seen a halt in the cycle of decline across the entire church. Indeed a number of "growth points" have emerged, and there has been slow but steady growth. What has been clear and consistent with our understanding of our ethos is that where there is quality leadership at all levels of the congregation, growth has been the consequence. Since that time eight new congregations have been established.
- There is greater learning among both clergy and laity. In many of our councils people are being trained as lay pastors and as elders, with

many other opportunities existing for development among the many critical areas of church life and witness.

- There is indeed greater mobilization of people, in that ten years ago our synod events could be held at any of our larger church buildings, whereas we are now forced to look at larger facilities elsewhere to hold these events.
- Greater levels of stewardship have been demonstrated. Between 1985 and 1995 our synodical budget moved from J$1.2 million to J$35 million, and in 2001 it was over J$60 million. This is testimony to significant strides in our stewardship response!
- The Cayman council had a gap of thirty years in which no one was offered for pastoral training. Currently there are four persons being trained. The church there took the time to determine, through a very open and honest debate, the affirmation of one church in two nations, and in support of this initiated the process that led to the appointment of a deputy general secretary located in Grand Cayman to provide leadership for the local people.

In spite of these positive developments, the renewal process has experienced some serious problems. The period 1985 to 1995 found the church employing more persons in its administration and training more persons at regional centres for its ministry and mission. The hope was that, with more persons engaged in the church's development, the resulting output would generate sufficient resources to finance that growth. However, the church life trend for that period suggests that the input did not produce the necessary output in the following core areas of the church's life.

Church structures: Although significant changes were made at the synodical and area council levels, at the level of the local congregation structures for ministry and mission remained static and heavy, unable to respond in a flexible and creative way to the concerns within their communities.

Worship: To a great extent, worship represents an uninspiring memorial to a past age rather than a reflection of the rich and diverse spiritual resources that our people offer in their response to God. New initiatives were undertaken to renew the liturgy and music. But again this represented a piecemeal approach to the problem. The renewal programme failed to excite and attract enough local congregations.

Leadership: Our clergy and elder model of managing the local congregation has not resulted in enough believers being motivated and released to participate in the ministry.

Mission: It must be noted, however, that it was during this period that the church made great strides in the sharing more of its human resources with the worldwide church.

Stewardship: Although the congregations responded to the synod's initiatives with increased giving they failed to "co-own" the programmes, and they remained just that – initiatives of the synod. Although creative steps were taken to invest resources to keep pace with expansion, the pace of development outstripped the resources available. The local congregations, which constitute the core source of financing for the development of the church, failed to grow at the required rate. The general stagnation in the national economy had a negative impact upon the synod's investment instruments. The end of that decade found the synod experiencing intense financial dislocation.

These areas of persistent weakening of the church's life and witness suggest that, at the core, the renewal process has not been sufficiently owned by the leaders and worshippers in the local congregations. Critical questions have been raised about the speed with which changes have been implemented, and the educational process used to get people onboard. Others argue that rapid structural changes which did not seem to be working have been dismantled even before in-depth evaluation of them has taken place. And there is an equally strong view that the tension between instant results and long-term strategic change is still in the balance. What is clear is that these issues are firmly on the table at the critical levels of the church, and form the basis for a strategic development plan currently being pursued.

Challenges

Imperatives for mission development

In spite of the union, the church continues to face issues of survival, diminishing members, money, influence and importance within a culture that is increasingly resistant to the gospel. Two contrasting developmental features dominate the church's current expression of ministry and mission. The first is its perennial struggle to come to terms with its inherited missionary model and pattern of ministry, and the second is the contemporary thrust to restructure and equip itself to become more responsive to mission challenges. The fundamental litmus test for the successful renewal of the united church must be evidence of a new and heightened understanding of its mission – an understanding that includes outreach services to the community as well as to its members. Another requirement for mission is that there must be a strong and growing core group of committed laity who are enthusiastic about the church's mission, and willing to make the sacrifices required to carry it out. It is their love for Christ and his church that motivates and equips them with a joyful spirit to serve others. They do so for Christ's sake!

The elements of change identified in the mission development of the united church over these 36 years enable us to celebrate those things that have proven valuable and meaningful and should be strengthened for the journey ahead. Some things have persistently demonstrated their inadequacies by being burdensome and unresponsive to the missionary calling of the United Church, and these should be reformed or abandoned. But in spite of all negative factors, there are within our community enough committed and available Christians who strongly believe that the United Church in Jamaica and the Cayman Islands has something special to offer to the witness of the gospel in Jamaica, the Cayman Islands and throughout the world.

The missionary calling to be a United church is tough and relentless. It requires that we be true to our core identity by rediscovering the unity that Jesus prayed for his disciples to experience: "Father, may they be one, so that the world may believe that you sent me" (cf. John 17:21). The call to unity – for a wholesome relationship with God and with one another – is for the sake of others! Only if others see us *living* as "good news", and being a blessing for others, will they take seriously the ministry and mission of the church.

Contemporary trends

Developments in the wider national and regional religious scene over the past 36 years since Jamaica received its independence have resulted in some fundamental changes which will affect the *ways of being church* in the new millennium. These developments include:

- the erosion of denominational affiliation as the central component in a congregation's identity;
- a significant increase in the numbers of Christians who identify their faith as Pentecostal or evangelical;
- higher expectations for anyone seeking to become a member of a local church;
- the impact of television on worship and preaching;
- contemporary Christian music, which is gradually marginalizing traditional church music;
- a significant increase in congregations who allow laity to "do" ministry while paid staff "manage the church";
- a shift from traditional Sunday school to the development of "discipling communities" embracing persons of all ages;
- the decentralization of theological education, making it more accessible to the whole people of God;
- the greater willingness of younger Christians to switch from one religious tradition to another;

- the societal demand for excellence in preaching, in meeting places and facilities, children's ministries, and training experiences for volunteers;
- the demand for small group ministries to meet needs not being met by the traditional church structures.

The most dominant challenge the church faces is the increasing demand for excellence in ministry. People are more and more dissatisfied with an average quality of ministry, with ministry which offers them limited inspiration and very limited choices in expressing their Christian faith. They want attractive choices in worship, learning, personal and spiritual growth, fellowship and involvement in ministry.[2]

The way forward

At the heart of the matter is a deep concern about the identity of the United Church. What does it stand for? What is it called to be and to do? Having embraced the identity of being a "united church", we have given priority to a relational ethos. The coming together of Christians from different church traditions becomes the springboard for new missionary obedience which involves taking risks to achieve the goal. Our identity and vocation is to be found in our understanding and practice of mission! The task is to enable our members, at all levels, to articulate clearly who we are and what we are about. This calls for continued evaluation and restructuring at the local and synodical levels.

Conclusion

Through its ongoing development plan the United Church in Jamaica and the Cayman Islands is attempting to rediscover and recommit itself to its mission mandate for the 21st century. As we attempt to heal the wounds of our suffering world we are cognisant of the continuing need to reshape our congregations so that they become more open, accessible, vulnerable and able to move beyond themselves, to reach out to those in need. The fundamental missionary vocation of the United Church will emerge as we incarnate the good news within our culture, in the customs, music and language of the people. We are indeed a church that was offered its mission by God, but practised it in a way which contradicted its true calling. We are challenged not so much to embrace the dominant culture and values of our society, we are challenged by Christ to become transforming and influencing agents, salt and light! Truly we have come a far way – yet in so many ways the journey has just begun.

Author's addendum

Since the Driebergen consultation a number of developmental shifts have taken place within the United Church of Jamaica and the Cayman Islands.

Pivotal among them has been a development strategy which includes the restructuring of our leadership at both the synodical as well as the local levels. The office of moderator has been redefined, with a stronger focus on pastoral care supported by a complementary structure at the regional levels through the area council chairs. The Cayman area council enjoys a greater level of autonomy through the office of deputy general secretary, now located in Grand Cayman. At the local level there is a comprehensive eldership training programme, which elders pursue before they are commissioned into office in order to ensure the delivery of quality and competent ministry and service within congregations.

There has been a deliberate focus on the church's missional journey with the community. In this respect, the Institute for Theological and Leadership Development has embarked on the delivery of a number of courses connecting people with the community, including guidance and counselling (targeting the young in our schools in holistic ways). Complementing this is a redesigned chaplaincy programme at the various institutional levels. A critical strategic development in this direction is the imminent establishment of a university, pulling together three United Church educational institutions, to provide cutting-edge programmes and courses at all levels. Another vital component of our interaction with the community is the ongoing establishment of counselling care centres throughout the church, to enable the delivery of services at the point where people are hurting.

At the heart of all this is our pursuit of ecumenical initiatives on leadership development: at the local level through our interaction and initiatives with the theological institutions; at the regional level through our leadership and involvement with the Caribbean and North America Council for Mission (CANACOM), Caribbean and North America area council (CANAC); and at the international level, where our own Roderick Hewitt provides leadership as the moderator of the Council for World Mission.

NOTES

[1] Reflection of the UCJCI study group on the CWM document "Perceiving Frontiers, Crossing Boundaries" (the report of the Partnership in Mission consultation of the Council for World Mission, 3-7 April 1995, D. Preman Niles).

[2] Lyle E. Schaller, "7 Trends Affecting You", Leadership Journal, *Christianity Today*, spring 1998.

Source Document

"The Missionary Calling of the United Church in the 21st Century: A Discussion Paper", Roderick R. Hewitt, 1999.

Resource Person

Maitland Evans, general secretary, United Church in Jamaica and the Cayman Islands.

A Case Study on the Relationship between Mission and Unity

The Uniting Church in Australia

TERENCE CORKIN

I have been asked to share with you some reflections on four topics that speak to the theme of the relationship between unity and mission:

1) how, in practice, United churches have pursued mission (is there a distinctive "United church" understanding of mission?);
2) whether, in fact, the union can be said to have enabled more effective mission;
3) how United churches can be more effective in mission in the future;
4) what advice in this area your church has for churches currently moving towards union.

My invitation to deliver this presentation says: "We hope your comments in these areas would open up a lively discussion at the consultation." On the strength of that invitation I will drop my usual mode of operation, which is to be very diplomatic and guard my words carefully. Rather, I will take the liberty of throwing out a few perspectives, some experience and "angles" on the issue. In sharing some candid comments, I hope this may enable you to connect your setting with our experience, and perhaps stimulate some reflection which will be helpful for you in your own place. Perhaps I should also say that the opinions expressed in this paper are my own and do not necessarily reflect the views of the Uniting Church in Australia (UCA) as such.

How United churches have pursued mission

The foundational document for the Uniting Church is the basis of union. Within it we find expressed the convictions of those who came into the union and which, hopefully in a non-legalistic way, continue to shape and inspire our identity as a Christian community.

Paragraph 3 of the basis says (among other things),

> Jesus of Nazareth announced the sovereign grace of God whereby the poor in spirit could receive God's love... In raising him to live and reign, God confirmed and completed the witness which Jesus bore to God on earth, reasserted claim over the whole of creation, pardoned sinners, and made in Jesus a representative beginning of a new order of righteousness and love.

> The church as the fellowship of the Holy Spirit confesses Jesus as Lord over its own life; it also confesses that Jesus is Head over all things, the beginning of a new creation, of a new humanity... The church's call is to serve that end: to be a fellowship of reconciliation, a body within which the diverse gifts of its members are used for the building up of the whole, an instrument through which Christ may work and bear witness to himself.

Fundamentally the UCA is deeply convicted of the significance of the incarnation: God was in Christ present to the world in a unique and decisive way. God's action in the world affirms the creation as the context for the revelation and mission of God. Mission therefore is inherently contextual; and any methodology of mission must be shaped by the context within which that mission is effected. As a way of working, therefore, I would not want to assert that there is a distinctively "United church way" of doing mission. Just as the mission of God in Jesus was effected in a way that was profoundly shaped by the context that we now call intertestamental Judaism, and the Greco-Roman culture within which it was located, so too God's mission through his body, the church, is shaped by its context.

Briefly I note that part of the distinctive context within which the UCA operates is a migrant community, one which dispossessed the indigenous people who were operating within the Asia-Pacific region. This context, as a setting for mission, is recognized in the basis when it says,

> It [the UCA] believes that Christians in Australia are called to bear witness to a unity of faith and life in Christ which transcends cultural and economic, national and racial boundaries, and to this end the Uniting Church commits itself to seek special relationships with churches in Asia and the Pacific. The Uniting Church declares its desire to enter more deeply into the faith and mission of the church in Australia, by working together and seeking union with other churches.

While I have said that union, by itself, does not inculcate a distinctive mission style or mode of operation, the fact that a union takes place in a particular context does impact upon the self-understanding and priorities of the church which comes into being. Or at least it should! For the UCA the impact has been a commitment to accommodating a wide variety of different cultures within its life. In honesty, I have to say we still struggle to enable those cultures to impact on the way we "do our business"; but we are committed to that struggle. In fact it is in the area of multicultural ministry that the UCA finds some of its most vibrant congregations, and where nearly all the new congregations entering the Uniting Church are to be found.

Has union actually fostered mission?

It would be a brave speaker at this conference who would suggest that the uniting of churches is no help to mission! Such a claim would fly in the face of the great prayer of Jesus "that they may be one" (John 17:21), which we so often quote in this kind of context. Nevertheless, I think we all know that becoming a united church is no "magic formula" for the resurgence and renewal of missionary endeavour and effectiveness.

I think that there were some unconscious mistakes made at the time of union in 1977, mistakes that perhaps reflect a subconscious assumption that uniting, of itself, would flow through to a greater effectiveness in mission. On 22 June 1977 I was a 20-year-old member of a self-sufficient congregation which had a minister to call its own. We were put into a parish that comprised seven congregations and five ministers. It was, frankly, an organizational and relational nightmare. But it was also a broadening experience that created opportunities for new ministries and relationships, compelled me to address many faith issues and generated some significant pooling of resources for ministry and mission. Of course the appreciation of, and sense of need for, these blessings would have varied from congregation to congregation.

My impression at that time, and in the subsequent years, was that throughout the first decade – and perhaps longer – of the Uniting Church a huge amount of energy was put into getting these congregations from the various uniting traditions to know each other, and to work together. A great deal of time was spent in developing a feeling of being part of a larger, cooperative group (the best methodologies for that were not always used, I might add).

My impression was, and remains, that a good deal of the energy and effort of the church was turned in on itself. It was as though (albeit unreflectively) we thought that if we could get on together, then the church would be more "effective" – whatever that means! Perhaps it was the latent belief that strong congregations, and denominational structures "doing more", would automatically facilitate the proclamation of the gospel. There is an abiding (I believe unfounded) confidence that if we keep the programmes and practices of the church going, then everything will "work out OK". In the late 1970s and the 1980s in Australia we were living that conviction out, by being over-fixated on the internal organizational interests of the church. This was a mistake born of a misplaced confidence that by maintaining and strengthening the church "system", the mission of God would be advanced.

In respect of the broader institutional life of the church, the bringing together of so many skilled and gifted people to lead and work with us was a wonderful focusing of "people resources". This greater pool of gifted people enhanced the structures of the church, and thus union was a great benefit – it is, after all, no crime to use people and financial resources efficiently! Church unions indeed facilitate this. Nevertheless, the trap for the church is to assert that the missional benefits of union are to be found in an ecclesiological version of economic rationalism and drives for efficiency. But in fact missional benefits do not arise from those sources; and to the extent that the UCA was seduced by these goals it overlooked likely sources of renewal in mission.

Being more effective in mission in the future

The third point addresses how United churches could be more effective in mission in the future. In making the above observations, the impression might easily be given that the UCA has not benefited significantly in its mission enterprise through the experience of union. This is, however, not so. And further, more significant, benefits might accrue to the mission of God in the future due to the union experiences of the Presbyterian, Methodist and Congregational churches in Australia in 1977. But before noting these I must make an observation or two.

Church union in Australia happened on the cusp of the most significant decline in rates of religious participation that Australia has ever seen. It happened after what had been a "golden period" for the institutional and congregational life of the churches in Australia. There are far too many factors to comment upon here, but suffice it to say that Australia has not been immune to the changing social circumstances, and the responses to them, which have led to the downward spiral of traditional mainline denominations across the Western industrialized world. Therefore it is not possible to assert confidently that the creation of the UCA has been effective in facilitating mission at a time when, by every measure, the connection of the church with the wider community, and rates of participation in the church, have declined. In so far as the union has enabled the church to maintain its traditional practices and resources for ministry and mission, during such a time of decline for mainline churches, the union has been very helpful. On their own – that is, had they remained separate – the uniting denominations would have been much more diminished than has been the case.

I wish now to assert very strenuously that the experience of uniting has laid a platform which places the UCA in a very strong position to adapt and respond to the new context in which the Christian community finds itself in Australia, in the early years of this century. If time permitted I would say more about how I believe the context of Australia is radically different today from that of forty or fifty years ago, and what that means for the way the church must operate. Here I will limit myself to sharing some of the experiences and discoveries which our history of uniting has brought us to.

First, one of the catch phrases of the UCA, drawn from the basis, is that we are a "pilgrim people always on the way". One of the greatest tensions in uniting is that you really have no choice but to change. This struggle means that the UCA has a large number of people – and many in leadership – who sit easy with the structures of the church: we know from experience that structures and regulations and organizational systems will not save the church. We know they are transient servants of the living God. Interestingly, those congregations which did not have to wrestle with bringing together different denominations into a parish are our least innovative. Generally speaking we dare not build ourselves a "permanent city" – because the experience of union has taught us that this, like all things in creation, decays and fades away.

We have found that our loyalty should be to Christ, and we have to be willing to put aside old patterns where they do not reflect or communicate the gospel. While people do not want change for its own sake, they do want structures which are adaptable, flexible, nimble. In a world of rapid change and multiple constituencies and mission fields, churches need to be adaptable. I think in our heart of hearts we know that we are a pilgrim people always on the way towards a promised goal; and that we do not have a continuing city; and we are thankful that we have Christ to feed us in word and sacrament and the Spirit that we will not lose the way (basis, para. 3). Union has taught us this – and it is good.

Second, we all know that denominations have their favourite emphases, either in doctrine or morals or other areas. When churches remain divided and such groups are kept apart it is easy to critique "the other", and even to doubt the quality and authenticity of their faith. However, when you bring different traditions together into the same church it is not so easy to do that! The experience of union has taught us that the unity of the church is not in dogma or morality or heritage or denominational practices. We spent a great deal of energy trying to create a united "character" for the UCA by crunching everyone into our preferred mould – but it did not work. Sadly, some are still trying. Yet more and more people are taking seriously the practical consequences of knowing that our unity as Christians can only be in Christ. It is this discovery, founded for us in the struggle to make sense of our unity in diversity, that is and/or will be the fountainhead of mission. Christ is the only one to whom we can point when asked: "What keeps you together? Why do you put up with each other?"

Christ can cope with our many stages of maturity, our differing theologies and practices and the varying quality and emphases of our ministry. And so should we – because such matters are not what makes Christians one. Indeed this capacity to cope with diversity and very different experiences of life fits well with a pluralistic world-view. At the end of the day, of course, we know that it is not a case of "anything goes" in the Christian life. However, if we can accept that people may be responsive to the call of the risen Christ even when they are not like us, then chances are they will stay connected to our communities of faith and have a better chance of maturing.

Third, the congregation that knows that its life and faith are founded exclusively on a relationship with Jesus Christ must be humble and gracious. Ultimately we are saved by grace. The experience of uniting can assist the discovery of grace and the emergence of a more gracious Christian community. I rather suspect that the witness to the gospel will be more effective if we live graciously and love people into the kingdom, rather than advocate a certain life-style, or theology, or the adoption of a particular cultural expression of the Christian life.

Fourth, the ecumenical disposition of the UCA membership is incredibly high. This is driven by our experience of union; and to the extent that the mission of the church is enhanced through ecumenical cooperation, then our experience of union is a factor in the effective mission of the church. We continue to strengthen relationships with many churches and find that persons from various denominations join the UCA.

Advice for churches moving towards union

What advice would I be presumptuous enough to give to other churches entering into union? On the basis of our experience I would offer four suggestions.

The first is to ensure that members of the different traditions which are entering the Uniting church have to meet and work together and, in the process, ensure that, wherever possible, they spend time talking about the things they value and why. We did not encourage a sharing about the values and convictions that lay behind our actions and statements, and so we frequently had conflict because we focused on outcomes rather than foundations. It sounds simple but it is easily overlooked: talk about your faith.

Second, we always said that uniting was not an end in itself but a foundation for mission. However, in a congregational context it is very easy to be seduced into spending a lot of time on "bedding down" the union. The practice of the church and congregations easily takes on the impression that "getting on with" these other, somewhat different Christians is the name of the game. I would recommend a strategy, including a general time-line, that identifies what is needed *relationally* as well as organizationally to move things along. (As an aside, if you can be using the same music resources in worship before uniting that will be a great help.)

Third, give thought to how your meetings and other processes can encourage people to be gracious towards one another. We have moved to a consensus style of decision-making rather than the argumentative parliamentary style. This has changed the tone of our meetings and the way we meet each other quite dramatically. If we could have had that operating at the time of union, I think it would have reduced the combative approach taken by some as they sought to establish the dominance of their tradition over others coming into the union.

Fourth and finally – be brave and expectant, and understand that the days are over when you will be able to stamp one single form of church life on to two or three groups coming together from different traditions. (You have to be brave, because it is a wild ride at times and one can wonder: How did I ever get into this?) And be expectant, because a new character, and insights, do arise that can refresh and refocus the church.

Earthen Vessels or God's Building?
The Identity of United and Uniting Churches

DAVID M. THOMPSON

Before any analysis of identity in United and Uniting churches is possible, something must be said about how the identity of any church, or even the church in general, is understood. The church is itself an object of faith as well as a social institution. To believe in the church is part of what it means to believe in God, understood within a trinitarian framework: the God whose Word was made flesh in Jesus of Nazareth also bestowed the Holy Spirit on those who put their faith in Jesus as the Christ; and that Spirit-filled community is the church. In this most elementary and fundamental sense, the identity of United and Uniting churches is no different from the identity of any other church. But that statement immediately identifies the problem. In the creed we say that we believe in "one, holy, catholic and apostolic church": what then are these separate church*es* of which we speak? The New Testament speaks of the church at Antioch, or Corinth, or Rome. Here the identity is that of church – the difference is one of place. So are we primarily concerned with identity or difference?

My intention in this paper is to concentrate on identity in a historical and social perspective.[1] I shall not attempt to develop an argument which draws on the psychological insights of Freud or Michel Foucault, though this could be done. Nor shall I speak for the most part in terms of the church's identity in Christ. At a fundamental theological level the church's identity is based on Christ; but it is a category mistake to use such theological language within a primarily historical discourse as an alternative to historical analysis, because it can too easily evade hard questions about social and institutional identity.

The reference to place is an important reminder that we still define churches by place, even if today the "place" is usually the nation. Even the Roman Catholic Church, by retaining the title of Pontifex Maximus taken over from the Roman empire, sustains a political or quasi-political dimension in its life and aspirations; and as we enter the third millennium we can see more clearly than before the profound difference between the ecclesiological and theological outlooks of those churches which are rooted west of the holy land, based in the Roman imperium which existed when Jesus himself lived, and of those churches which are rooted east of the holy land and grew from the beginning in a completely different political and religious environment. Such churches rarely dreamed of – and even more rarely experienced – the possibility that their whole society might be officially Christian. The challenge to reconsider some quite basic assumptions in ecclesiology derived from this difference is considerable. That challenge is the more important because this difference antedates the division between East and West as traditionally understood, that is in Roman imperial terms; and it therefore requires an awareness of a Christian tradition very differently expressed from those of Europe, both West and East.

The context for identity

Place is another way of talking about context; and the varying contexts for United churches shape their identities in different ways. All the United churches formed thus far are Protestant. But they are to be found in at least three different politico-ecclesiastical contexts.

Politico-ecclesiastical contexts for unity

The first, mostly in Germany, are those unions of Lutherans and Reformed to form a single Landeskirche alongside the Roman Catholic church. Such unions, mainly dating from the 19th century, represent Protestant solidarity in particular areas, though political changes since 1866 have modified boundaries in some cases. Their identity is bound up with the place, since any further change would involve either a wider national Protestant identity or some kind of rapprochement with the Roman Catholic Church.[2]

A second context is that of the British Commonwealth and the USA. United churches in Canada, the United States, Great Britain and Australia all derive from a context of religious tolerance and diversity, and involve partial groupings of the patchwork of Protestant churches. Only in Great Britain is the situation affected by the formal establishment of particular churches. Thus far the Church of England has not found it possible to engage in a union with another church; the Church of Scotland in its current form is the result of a reunion of different presbyterian churches, though somewhat later than corresponding unions in most other former British dominions.

A third context is that of Asia and Africa, for the most part postcolonial situations where the inheritance was one of missionary diversity. In the Churches of South India, North India, Pakistan and Bangladesh, the range of churches involved has been greatest, including the Anglican church. Here too the context of Christian mission in a multifaith world has been paramount, and also the context of new nations. But for the most part, the participants are those churches deriving from British missionary work. Lutherans have not been involved (except in Pakistan), nor American Methodists. This certainly reflects different missionary strategies, and probably also different national perspectives. Elsewhere in East Asia and Africa there has been more American involvement but not Anglican. While it is certainly wrong to draw direct links between ecumenical efforts and nationalist and anti-colonial movements, the context of building a new nation makes this different from the two previous Western contexts.

Memories as a context for unity

Two points may be made about these different contexts. One is that there is a variety of different "memories" at work in them.

In the first type of situation, the essential memory is that of the Reformation divide, and the impulse to Protestant unity is mobilized by the sense of difference from the Roman Catholic Church. To a significant extent since Vatican II this context has changed, though at different speeds in different places. How, then, is the identity reconceived in the changing situation?

In the second type of situation, the essential memory is that of internal division within Protestantism, complicated to some extent by the tendency of the Anglican churches since the 19th century to understate their Reformed inheritance, particularly the Calvinist theology which lies behind the Thirty-Nine Articles of the Church of England. On the other hand, the 18th-century tension between Arminian and Calvinist evangelicals has faded significantly, facilitating unions involving Methodists, Congregationalists and Presbyterians in Canada and Australia (though not, as yet, in England). To this extent, therefore, the memory of that tension has been overcome. (One of the more intriguing moments in the recent formal conversations between the Church of England and the Methodist church came when the Methodist representatives had to face the situation that there remain within the Church of England some whose commitment to a Calvinist position on predestination is just as firm as, if not firmer than, that of some of those within the other English Free churches.)

In the third type of situation, there may still be strong memories of different missionary traditions, depending on the nature of the ongoing relationship with missionary societies in the Western churches; but the memories, positive or negative, of colonialism are likely to be just as significant. Indeed the success of the church may be proportional to the extent to which it has been able to rid itself of the label of "the white man's religion". Here the fact was very important that Protestant missions were much more hesitant about indigenization than historically Roman Catholic missions had been. Whereas Pope Gregory the Great told St Augustine of Canterbury not to destroy the temples of the idols in England but rather to destroy the idols, to cleanse the temples and erect new altars to the true God,[3] later evangelical missionary activity from the 18th century drew a much sharper distinction between the old places of worship and the new. Furthermore, the relationship of the United church to the "new nation" in post-colonial situations is also significant.

United churches in relation to the secular power

The relationship of the church in general, and United churches in particular, to the secular power is the second main point to be made. The church cannot avoid taking a position on the place of the state. Despite the long historical tradition (based on Old Testament precedent and the historic action of the Roman emperor, Constantine) in which the church offers, on varying terms, some kind of sacred recognition of the legitimacy of the state, the refusal of Christians, like Jews, to worship the gods of the state leads either to some kind of toleration of a special position or to conflict. The gods of post-Enlightenment states tend to assume an appropriately secular form, but even sociologists and political scientists now recognize that the religious cannot simply be excluded from an account of society. In fact the enthusiasm of apparently intelligent people for New Age religious phenomena, and the wish in some Western countries for "pagan" groups to be officially recognized as religious, shows that the Enlightenment notion of progress in which "primitive" religions would be abandoned was an illusion; similarly the idea of an "absolute religion"[4] has to be abandoned as well.

How then do we evaluate different religious traditions in a multifaith society? Can it be a sufficient defence of social customs which we regard as indefensible on moral or philosophical grounds – for example, certain attitudes to women and children, ways of making or breaking marriage, and others – to say that they are justified by a person's religious convictions? Put more sharply, just how universal is the Universal Declaration of Human Rights, and are all rights compatible with one another?

More important, however, is the political point. The state is the basic preserver of law and order, and therefore of internal peace. This is the main reason for the respect given to the state (in so far as the use of that term is not anachronistic) in the New Testament. But the appropriate role of the state vis-a-vis different Christian groups or different religious groups is bound to be a matter of Christian reflection. Many Christians still believe that the state cannot (and should not) be neutral in relation to Christianity, usually because they believe that the state should itself endorse and uphold Christian values. Yet if we hold to another principle enunciated by Bede in his account of the conversion of the English, namely that King Ethelbert encouraged but did not compel his subjects to be converted "for he had learned from his instructors and leaders to salvation, that the service of Christ ought to be voluntary, not by compulsion",[5] then we will not rush to argue for an explicitly Christian state in a multifaith society. Indeed, part of the identity of a United church might lie in an appropriate reticence in demanding that the state should stand for what are distinctive characteristics of the church. Pragmatically this strengthens the moral position of the church in arguing for a similar religious neutrality in states where the majority religion is different from Christianity.

The churches in relation to nationalism

There is a wider issue here, which I do not have time to develop, about the relation of the churches to nationalism. In the last twenty years there has been a vigorous debate about the origins and nature of nationalism, with essentially modernist interpretations, based on capitalism and its application to printing being offered by Ernest Gellner and Benedict Anderson; and a broader interpretation, giving full weight to the significance of Christianity and the translation of the Bible into the vernacular as a driving force for the development of written language, being offered by Adrian Hastings.[6] Each author has specific expertise in nationalism in three different parts of the world (central Europe, South-east Asia and Africa) so there is no simple choice between one view and another. Historically, the churches have been deeply involved in sustaining national self-consciousness, both for good and for ill. There is here an inescapable tension between "the scandal of particularity" – the incarnational principle that the church takes root in a particular local situation to which it has to speak – and the ministry of reconciliation, whereby the church has to demonstrate that "there is no longer Jew or Greek, there is no longer slave or free, there is no longer male and female; for all of you are one in Christ Jesus" (Gal. 3:28).

Furthermore it is highly significant that, apart from the Roman Catholic Church, all the main Christian traditions have located decision-making at national, or sometimes sub-national level, with world manifestations of particular traditions having a consultative role only. This is reflected in the fact that membership of the World Council of Churches was based on national churches rather than Christian world communions from the first draft constitution prepared at Utrecht in 1938;[7] and the passage of time has only heightened the significance of this, even if the question is now being raised again. United churches are no different from others in being drawn into decisions about how they relate their identity to that of the nation in which they are set. The difficulties, for example, of drawing all the Lutheran churches in the United States whose origin lay in different European countries into one church illustrate the point; just as the fact that British Methodists in South India became part of the Church of South India, whereas American Methodists did not, illustrates it in a different way. Sometimes there may be good, and sometimes less good, reasons for wanting to retain links with the churches from which missionaries and emigrants came.

Ways of understanding identity

Resources – past, present, future – for understanding a united identity

I turn now to various ways of approaching an understanding of the identity of United and Uniting churches.[8] The simplest way of understanding identity is in terms of a coming together of the component traditions; a United church inherits each of the traditions which made it up. Whilst this is self-evidently the case in general, it is much more difficult to realize in particular. Local congregations are likely to be related primarily to one of the component traditions, unless they are the result of local unions. Even then there can be no guarantee that the balance of membership is in any sense "representative" (whatever that might mean) of the larger whole.

Furthermore, if for any reason the local union was in some sense forced, the memories of it may not be positive. Different churches approach the local "rationalization" of congregations in different ways. I remember one Methodist congregation in Cambridge which was required to close and join another; but a significant portion of the membership of the closed congregation joined the nearby United Reformed Church rather than journey into the city centre. On the other hand, I can think of local unions within the United Reformed Church (Congregational/Presbyterian, Congregational/Church of Christ, and occasionally all three) which have been entered into with enthusiasm and which have reinvigorated the congregations concerned. However, thirty years on (and perhaps sooner) it no longer makes sense – even if it were desirable – to continue to think primarily in terms of the congregations which originally came together. So what is the identity of the united congregation? It can show itself in little ways – in what hymnbook is used, in whether there is a tradition of congregational participation in the reading of scripture and the leading of prayer, in the frequency of the celebration of holy communion, in the kind of fund-raising events which are organized. Are these simply contingent, or are they subtle ways in which particular traditions survive?

A different approach is to forget the pre-existing traditions and concentrate upon the founding documents of the United church. Most United churches have an equivalent to the basis of union of the United Reformed Church, even if the title is slightly different or if it includes two or three documents rather than one. Such a document sets out basic theological principles and establishes a church structure in varying degrees of detail. At some point there will probably be a reference to shared credal formulations (e.g. the Apostles' and Nicene Creeds, and possibly other historical formularies as well) and perhaps to ecumenical commitments such as those entailed in membership of the World Council of Churches. If ecclesial identity is primarily based on such founding documents, the earlier denominational traditions are relativized. In any "identity crisis" the appeal will typically be to the new rather than to what preceded it. The pre-union history and tradition is therefore marginalized in favour of the new identity. Such a strategy has obvious advantages: it is a constant reminder that something new has been ventured upon; it is intended to avoid a constant looking back to the past.

With the passage of time as pre-union memories fade, such an appeal might be expected to become second nature. However, things are rarely so simple. Christianity is an inexorably historical religion, and memories are not so easily erased. Furthermore, suppressed traditions can sometimes surface in unexpected ways; they can even be invented or reinvented – indeed the mistaken invocation of particular traditions can be more troublesome than the traditions themselves (for example, some interpretations of the Reformation insight into the significance of the priesthood of all believers).

In any case, the founding documents of any church are rarely sufficient for the new theological or moral situations which the passage of time makes it necessary to encounter. Were it not for the sanctification offered by a particular kind of theological tradition, it might seem absurd to attempt to resolve modern questions of sexuality or interfaith dialogue by reference to texts about sexual behaviour or false gods which are some 2500 or more years old. In fact, the history of the church offers a more diverse set of traditions than this as a resource; but this exposes a sharp tension which has to be faced by any who are involved in union negotiations – the tension between those matters which can and must be agreed, and those where there needs to be a guarantee of openness to new things, or old things understood in new ways.

Different again from either of the first two, though related to them, is what might be called identity through communal memory. This is the kind of identity which is much more like family than theological tradition. Sometimes it may even misrepresent a theological tradition. In some communities, the membership of a congregation is rather like an extended family, with the strengths and weaknesses that such a situation brings. But even in larger communities communal memory can be very important. For example, I have long been convinced that in England there are significantly different religious dynamics in those communities where there is only one church, those where there are two, and those where there are more than two. Where there is only one church, it is likely to be the "established" church of the community, regardless of the official legal status of establishment. Where there are two churches, one may be the "established" church and the other, in some sense, a reaction against it. Where there are more than two churches, more than a simple polarization between "established" and "non-established" is needed to define the identity of each. But when churches are considered as regional or national entities, it is clear that they are likely to contain congregations from all, or at least two, of the three situations described. In the wider context, the identity characteristic of the pluralist situation is likely to be normative; and indeed this is the character of many theological traditions.

But from a practical point of view local memories will always be important. Where United churches have achieved their union by some reconciliation of memories (because in the past there had been an actual breaking apart), it may be possible to move forward to a changed relationship. Where there has not been such a reconciliation, such memories may be a significant obstacle in achieving any wider unity. For example, some would say that a nostalgic memory of the glories of the Welsh Revival in 1904-1905 has made it more difficult for Welsh non-conformity to come to terms with its radically changed situation by the end of the 20th century.

Fourthly, identity might be based on future hopes and expectations. At first sight this may seem a rather curious basis for identity – something which has not happened, rather than something which has. Yet most United churches actually hope that their union will be the basis of something larger and wider. Indeed the phrase "Unit*ing* church" is intended to mark that provisional character very clearly. There is no doubt that at its founding in 1972 the United Reformed Church in England and Wales did not expect to remain unchanged for very long; although it has been broadened in 1981 and 2000, the wider goal of a united church including Anglicans and Methodists has so far remained elusive.[9] In Australia, Canada and New Zealand there have been similar disappointments, though in the first two countries Methodists have been involved in the United churches formed: in New Zealand no United church was formed, though a number of cooperating parishes were. But church life cannot be planned over five to ten years on the basis that the church may not exist in that form at the end of the period. Questions such as provision for and training of ministers, policy over the planting of new congregations, strategies for youth and children's work or care of the aged – all require organizational responses today rather than tomorrow; and whilst the hope of a wider union may reasonably be kept on the table, it cannot in most cases dictate policy. So what kind of interim justification for the United church is offered? Here future hope, despite its rhetorical appeal, may be a source of paralysis.

Lived identity: the interplay of conviction and experience

Finally, therefore, there is what might be called the "lived identity" of a United church. All unions involve agreements over what were previously regarded as differences. Some indeed may have been differences which no longer had practical significance (such as the Calvinist/Arminian divide mentioned earlier), but they are unusual.[10] Some lie at the heart of the church's life – baptism, eucharist and ministry, for example; others relate to the structure of the church's organization and practical points like the payment of stipends; yet others may be related to social class or ethnicity. The lived identity of a United church involves manifesting diversity with integrity.[11] Let me illustrate this from the experience of the United Reformed Church.

One important feature of the United Reformed Church after 1981 was its accommodation of two convictions about the practice of baptism. Even before 1972, when Churches of Christ were observers at the Congregational-Presbyterian conversations, the joint committee agreed to draft its paragraph on baptism in such a way that at a future point it would not be necessary to delete anything, but only to add more. (This was a small but important decision.) In the negotiations between 1972 and 1977 we realized that we were concerned with differences of conviction as much as differences of practice; and so we drafted the revised paragraph in terms of respecting different convictions – between parents who did and did not wish their children to be baptized, and between ministers who were and were not prepared to administer infant baptism. Furthermore, the church recognized its dual obligation to parents and ministers, so that a minister's unwillingness to baptize could not be a reason for the parents' wish for baptism being refused; thus there was a commitment that another minister be invited to conduct the baptism.

The denial of the possibility of rebaptism was another way in which convictions were respected. Thus the paragraph on baptism – the longest in the basis of union – became both a statement about different patterns of Christian initiation, and also about ways in which differences of conviction were respected. On the whole the agreement has worked well. There is a greater sense of a freedom to choose for all parents; several congregations have included baptisteries for total immersion in church rebuilding projects; and only a small number of ministers (and not all ex-Churches of Christ ministers) have exercised the right not to baptize infants. A genuine unity in diversity has been achieved. Furthermore, this bridging of the "baptist" divide has also made the United Reformed church more hospitable to Baptist ministers and Local Ecumenical Partnerships with Baptist churches (though some local united congregations date back to the 19th century). The removal of an expectation that all parents will have their children baptized has not led to the collapse of infant baptism or believers' baptism; it has not resolved the dilemma facing ministers and elders' meetings who receive requests for baptism from parents with little or no regular contact with the church; but it has shown that many of the dire consequences predicted from the change (and sometimes used previously, on both sides, as reasons against change) have not materialized.

However, some matters which are related less directly to respect for others' convictions have proved more difficult. One example, related to the issue of baptism, is the question of children and communion. Although the general assembly has not formulated a policy which is binding on local congregations, there has nevertheless been a tendency on the part of those who advocate the admission of children to communion before confirmation and admission to the full privileges and responsibilities of membership to assume that children will have been baptized, despite the fact that the church's policy on baptism does not guarantee this. Alternatively, there has been a readiness to admit the unbaptized to communion without sufficient reflection on the ecumenical implications of such a policy in relation to sacramental practice in general.

Another example might be the frequency of holy communion. The Churches of Christ celebrated communion weekly. I only know of two United Reformed congregations to have adopted that policy since union, apart from local unions involving former Churches of Christ, namely the two Cambridge city centre churches – and one has subsequently discontinued it; though some congregations have increased the frequency to fortnightly. Nor have I ever had much sense that anyone not from a Churches of Christ tradition felt that this was a practice which the union of 1981 laid upon the church at large to consider, which may be why some former Churches of Christ members are happiest in Local Ecumenical Partnerships which also involve the Church of England. Furthermore, although non-stipendiary ministry was introduced as part of the union with Churches of Christ, the small numbers offering for that ministry make it difficult even to provide communion monthly in some districts without invoking the provision for lay presidency authorized by the district council; this is a great change from the situation in former Churches of Christ where nearly all congregations would have two or three ministers or elders ordained to preside at communion.

Nevertheless, the United Reformed Church manifests unity and diversity in different ways. For example, although the structure of the church specifies the functions of synods and districts, different synods (and different districts within the same synod) organize their life and the pattern of their meetings in different ways. By contrast, all ministers are paid the same stipend (apart from those with special synod or national responsibilities), and this is organized through the national church on the basis of contributions collected from local churches via districts and synods. It is the district's responsibility to provide ministry to the local churches within its oversight. Similarly, there is a nationally organized way in which ministers are introduced to congregations. Advertising and competitive stipends are not allowed. The significance of this achievement is considerable, when one recalls the discrepancy between Congregational and Presbyterian ministers' stipends in 1972 and the relative health of the two pension funds at that time. I have often said that the one point at which it seemed to me most likely that the Congregational-Presbyterian talks would fail was over ministers' stipends; but the will to succeed was greater!

A key quality in what I have described is mutual respect. This is also seen in a quite different area, that of culture. The United Reformed Church in the British context has been since 1981 (and even more so since 2000) one church in three nations: England, Wales and Scotland. Sensitivity to this has been important in the life of the church. The patterns and assumptions of church life in the three nations are significantly different; and the union of 2000 recognized that in certain circumstances the English synods of the church, although they constitute the majority, might need to allow the national synods of Wales and Scotland to act in different ways. Furthermore, even within England the size and distribution of the church varies between different parts of the country, and this is one reason for different ways of working. The case study on Ghanaians within the United Reformed Church offered at this consultation also indicates one way in which the church has sought to respond to wider changes in the ethnic balance of the United Kingdom, which affect all the British churches. The reference in this consultation to the position of immigrant churches reminded me that 19th-century English Presbyterianism was often a church of Scottish and Irish immigrants, which is why, for example, a Burns Night[12] may still be a significant social occasion and identity marker. Scots were also prominent in northern Congregationalism and in Churches of Christ; and this is a further reminder that geographical mobility (which is often seen as a factor weakening the strength of the British churches in the 19th century) actually strengthened certain non-conformist churches.

This mutual respect was, in a real sense, enhanced for the initial generation of those involved in union by an awareness that they were dying in order to live in a new form. Arthur MacArthur, formerly general secretary of the Presbyterian Church of England, has often referred to the impact made upon him by the explanation given by the church's lawyer of the legal processes necessary to inaugurate the union: the uniting churches would legally die, to be replaced by a new united church.[13] In this perspective it is often easier to see the necessity of making certain sacrifices; but one's readiness to do so is easily weakened by the sense, or fear, that others are making a lesser sacrifice than one's own. It is also worth noting in passing that in any church union negotiation there is an inestimable value in having legal advisers who are prepared to work out how they can make possible what the negotiators want to achieve, rather than those who simply tell them what they can and cannot do.

The essential point about this "lived identity", therefore, is that it marks the way in which being "United Reformed" is different from what it was to be Congregational, Presbyterian or Churches of Christ. Furthermore, when it is remembered not only that no one under the age of 35 has a significant personal memory of those "former days", but also that many have joined the United Reformed Church from other church backgrounds altogether, it is clear that the identity of this United church is more than the sum of its parts, and it is not just based on founding documents or future hopes. It is simply United Reformed. Even more simply, it is Christian.

Theologically, however, there is an opportunity for United churches which has probably not been exploited to the full. Many such churches offer some kind of statement of faith in contemporary terms in their founding documents. Only rarely have these statements been used as theological resources. There has been some reflection within the Uniting Church in Australia on its own statement,[14] but the majority of these statements, even when fiercely argued over at the time of their formulation, have become historic documents – in the unremembered rather than memorable sense of that term. Yet these statements, and the broader documents in which they are set, ought to be the basis for future theological reflection, precisely to test the extent to which they do faithfully reflect the faith of the church through the ages in a way which communicates to the contemporary world. In this way they too could become part of the "lived identity"of the church

Memories and majorities

I have referred to memory several times, and I want to develop this further. The importance of memory is self-evident. In a unique way memory is constitutive of personal identity. Someone who has lost his or her memory does not know who he or she is. This is the most distressing aspect of Alzheimer's disease to the relatives of the sufferer, though often the person concerned does not seem too troubled. Although the analogy is not precise, what is true of personal identity is also true of group identity. Certainly for the church, memory lies at the heart of its being: the command to "do this in memory of me" relates the church intimately to Christ at every celebration of the Lord's supper; and Christian prayer to God characteristically recalls acts of God in previous ages.

There is a difference between intra- and inter-generational memory. By this I mean the difference between what can be remembered within a single lifespan or the lifespan of a group (this being intra-generational), and what is passed on from one person or generation to the next (inter-generational). Intra-generational memories of division or conflict are particularly difficult to heal. Those involved in an experience of division, even if – perhaps particularly if – it was a division in order to unite, find it more difficult to overcome that memory than does the next generation. Inter-generational memories, however, are not less significant because they are less immediate. Indeed, in some ways they can be even more difficult to heal because they have hardened with age. Moreover, whilst it is undoubtedly correct theologically to say that unity is God's gift and that God gives healing, such theological correctness can always be used as an excuse for human inaction. People are called upon to act in a way that is reconciling: through such actions God's gift of reconciliation is made known.

This point about intra- and inter-generational memory is crucial for issues like the attitudes to non-participants in any union, and also for the awareness of theological traditions. If differences of opinion have developed over the wisdom or appropriateness of a particular union scheme, it is especially difficult for those who take the negative view to change their minds. First, the fact that they were not in favour of the union scheme suggests an unwillingness to change. But secondly, there is a tendency for those who favour union to be depicted as "betraying" their

heritage; hence any later move in the same direction shares in the "betrayal".

The stakes are always higher for opponents than for supporters of a particular proposal. Hence although most union schemes provide for non-participating congregations to join subsequently, typically not many do so. Some may wait to see which way the majority moves and then follow it; but most who stay out do so from conviction. Within the first generation there will rarely be found many who wish to change their mind. Subsequently attitudes may soften; but in the first instance the primary task is to resume good relations rather to contemplate reunion. There is a real sense in which a division over entering a union scheme mirrors earlier times of schism, and needs to be recognized as such. This is not an argument for movement only when a vote is unanimous, but it is an acknowledgment of the realities of broken fellowship. Even if the links did not seem very strong to begin with, the breaking of them makes a difference.

This in turn raises the question of what defines a "majority". The legal requirements are historically conditioned, and not necessarily the same from country to country. In Great Britain the pattern of expected majorities has been set by statute, following the Free Church of Scotland case of 1904. The attempt of the Free Church of Scotland and the United Presbyterian Church to unite in 1900 on the basis of church decisions alone, without any involvement of parliament, led to a legal challenge by the minority in the Free Church, who claimed that the United Free Church had abandoned certain basic principles of the former Free Church. The case went on appeal to the House of Lords as the highest court in the land, which ruled in favour of the minority and awarded all the Free Church's property (church buildings, manses and so on) to them. Since this was unworkable in practice, parliament was persuaded to legislate for an appropriate allocation between the United Free Church and the continuing Free Church. Nevertheless this led the United Methodist Church, when it was formed in 1907, to seek an enabling act of parliament, which specified that majorities of 75 percent should be obtained at various levels of the churches' governing bodies. This precedent was followed for the reunion of the Church of Scotland in 1929 and the reunion of British Methodism in 1932. The Free Church of Scotland case therefore demonstrated that in Britain no church was completely "free" as far as the law was concerned, forcing a reappraisal of church-state relations in all churches.

The legal provisions for the formation of the United Reformed Church in 1972 reflected two further sophistications in the process. On the question of majorities it was successfully argued that it would be unjust for a quarter of the smaller churches on either side to obstruct a decision that had the support of three-quarters of the total membership; hence the majority required was two-thirds of the number of congregations representing three-quarters of the total membership. The second point reflected differing ecclesiologies. It was argued that in a presbyterian polity the expectation was that congregations would act in accordance with the majority view of the church; hence in the Presbyterian Church of England it was necessary for a congregation to obtain a 75 percent vote in favour of staying out of the union, rather than in favour of going in. On the other hand, since a congregational polity is essentially voluntary, in the Congregational Union of England and Wales it was necessary for congregations to obtain a 75 percent majority in favour of joining the union.

Perhaps it is not surprising that no mainland congregations of the Presbyterian Church of England failed to join, whereas the Congregational Union split four ways – those who joined the United Reformed Church, those who formed the Congregational Federation, those who formed an Evangelical Fellowship of Congregational Churches, and those who joined no wider grouping but found it necessary to have some means of acting together in order to secure the share of corporate assets that were their due. Obviously two-thirds of Congregational churches representing three-quarters of the total membership did vote in favour of union, otherwise nothing would have happened. But the aftermath of the union, though it received little attention from the majority at the time, did leave a number of problems, particularly in situations where congregations which had worked together for many years now found themselves apart, and yet only partly apart. For so long as the generation which was involved in the division remained in positions of leadership on all sides, it was difficult to put those memories aside; and some personal animosities lasted for a long time. Former Presbyterians, precisely because they had not been involved in such a messy situation, often found it easier to make reconciling moves than former Congregationalists.

So does the sense of being a United church last more than a generation? I have referred to the reunions that produced the Church of Scotland in 1929 and the Methodist Church in Great Britain, formed in 1932. Seventy years later they are usually no longer regarded from the "outside" as United churches. Yet the traditions which they united and the difficulties which they faced were no less real because the polity was the same. Indeed, the recurrent Methodist tendency to interpret its history and theological tradition predominantly in terms of the Wesleyan majority, rather than of the significant but different Primitive and United Methodist streams within its history, still provokes irritation among some. Similarly, it would be interesting to know how far the United Church of Canada, which is older than either of the two British churches just mentioned, still regards its defining characteristic as being a United church (rather than, for example, as being a liberal Protestant church from which any tendencies to a conservative confessionalism have been excluded because they were represented by those Presbyterians who stayed out).

This reminds us of two points. First, there needs to be a self-conscious recollection of the responsibility within a United church to respect differences of conviction; secondly, this is easier when there is an ongoing process of realizing wider unity. However, even if the church were fully united, its unity is only sustained by those qualities of interpersonal relationships which are emphasized so regularly in the Epistles (e.g. Eph. 4:2).

Relations with other churches

I turn now to the ecumenical context of United churches: first, the relation of United churches to other churches of whatever tradition; secondly, the relation of United churches to other United churches; and thirdly, the relation of United churches to remnants left behind following the consummation of the immediate union process.

Sometimes United churches may be tempted to feel a sense of superiority in their relations to other churches. Even if this were justified, which on the whole is unlikely, it is tactically unwise and theologically inappropriate. Yet any United church has gone through a significant process of reflection, theological turmoil and often conflict in order to come into being. It is natural, then, that there should be a feeling of excitement and indeed enthusiasm about the union, which is not shared by those outside the process. Sometimes the other churches to which a United church has to relate may be former partners who decided to go no further, or those who chose not to become involved in the discussions. This is another example of the bundle of memories which accompany any movement towards union.

Furthermore all unions so far achieved are partial, even though some have been more comprehensive than others (for example, those in South Asia). This means that although some issues have been tackled and, as best as may be, resolved in United churches, others may have been quite deliberately avoided. One of the best examples of the attempt to tackle an issue which it was not necessary to face was the discussion in the preparations for the Uniting Church in Australia of the possibility of introducing bishops by a link with the Church of South India. For various reasons this possibility was not pursued; but it is a reminder to all United churches that their range thus far is limited. On the other hand, the Roman Catholic and Orthodox churches may see United churches as an essentially Protestant phenomenon, neither requiring nor justifying special treatment by comparison with other Protestant churches.

In the end the main thing which United churches have to offer in their relation to other churches is themselves, as they are. They offer a commitment to the unity of the church and a readiness to be renewed in the interest of wider unity. A rather different question is the relationship with churches that have not taken part in the ecumenical movement hitherto – various evangelical churches, Pentecostal churches, house churches or community churches. Here it is important to recognize that the circle of the church is never closed, but always opening out; and there is a challenge for the whole ecumenical movement in this area in so far as these groups have often hitherto had little ecumenical involvement, except at a local level.

The relationship with other United churches has been wrestled with over many decades. This consultation and its predecessors testify to the fact that, whereas United churches have resisted temptations to form any kind of worldwide organization, they do feel a continuing need to consult and meet together. For some of the reasons which I have discussed already, there is no necessary commonality between United churches such as that which ties churches of the same denominational tradition together. On the other hand, there is a common commitment to the goal of unity, including a wider unity than that which United churches have already attained. Equally, there has been a commitment to the World Council of Churches as the primary forum for the ecumenical journey; and United churches have a particular concern about any changes in overall ecumenical policy which presume that denominational churches are the norm and United churches are somehow exceptional. United churches have a continuing question about their relationship with Christian world communions, to which I shall return in the last section.

Finally, there is the question of relationships with continuing remnants. I have noted that it is probably inevitable that it will take a generation for the pain of the initial division to be overcome. Formal relationships may be resumed much earlier. The first exchange of representatives between the United Reformed Church and the Congregational Federation Assemblies took place in 1982 – ten years after the union of 1972. Perhaps the hardest thing to grasp is that there is likely to be a greater sense of welcome and wish for reconciliation from the Uniting church than from those who stay outside; and it may not be easy for those in the Uniting church to appreciate that their two positions are not symmetrical. The remnant is bound to be a minority. Hence the whole tangle of majority-minority relationships comes into play, something

which Christians so easily under-estimate or ignore. After a division, the welcome from the majority can easily be seen by the minority as a threat. Prospectively, the relationship can be very different: one of the outstanding features of the negotiations for union between the United Reformed Church and the Churches of Christ in Great Britain and Ireland between 1972 and 1979 was that the marked disparity in size between the two groups never entered into the discussions, or affected the basis on which decisions were reached. Even after 1981 members of the former Churches of Christ seemed to exercise a disproportionate influence in district councils of the United Reformed Church in those places where they were present.

One issue emphasized by opponents of organic union is whether the existence of remnant groups nullifies the point of the ecumenical process in the first place. One might, for example, observe that in the late 1960s there existed the Presbyterian Church of England, the Congregational Union of England and Wales, and the Churches of Christ in Great Britain and Ireland; whereas in the late 1980s there existed the United Reformed Church, the Congregational Federation, an Evangelical Fellowship of Congregational Churches, the Fellowship of Churches of Christ, together with some Congregational churches and Churches of Christ which did not join any of the new groupings. In other words instead of three churches there were now four, plus some congregations which do not belong anywhere. So how has the cause of ecumenism been advanced? It is a real question, which it is too easy to evade.

My own view, which is admittedly biased, is that this is not just a question about ecumenism; it is a question about ecclesiology and about the nature of evangelicalism. For what is at issue here is the nature of the church. Is the doctrine of the absolute independence of the local congregation ecclesiologically tenable or not? If it is tenable, then the consequence will continue to be separate groupings of independent congregations, and the total number of such groupings is relatively immaterial. Furthermore, if it is held that evangelicalism entails the independence of the local congregation, which is not a unanimous view but not uncommon, then that also will have a fissiparous tendency. From this perspective, whilst the ecumenical movement may be regarded as a rearrangement of the deck chairs on the *Titanic*, at least no new deck chairs have really come into existence. The argument that 1+1+1 = 4+ rather than 1, and is therefore counterproductive (the unspoken but implied consequence), is to that extent misleading.

There needs to be a more sustained engagement with the issue of independency in relation to ecclesiology. For many the issue seems clear when the topic of discussion is the local congregation; though even here there is a difference between those for whom independence means that they can raise their own funds to support their own minister without needing to consider the relative need of their congregation and others, and those for whom independence means that they are allowed gradually to dwindle on their own without having the opportunity to appeal for or to receive the help of others. Among the 20th-century British Free churches independency declined in attractiveness as memberships declined, and all the denominations which formally espouse independency have ways of subverting it in practice. In parts of the world where churches are growing, independency retains the attractiveness of laissez-faire capitalism. But if one moves from the local congregation and discusses the relationship of dioceses or provinces, and particularly the relationship of nations, then the issue of the appropriate level for local autonomy assumes a wider relevance. Subsidiarity offers a different way into some of these issues, one which deserves exploration across a wider field. There is no evidence to suggest that churches with centralized decision-making and law-enforcement systems are able to manifest the life of the gospel more clearly; their temptations are simply different.

United churches and the church universal

Can/should/must United churches claim the inheritance of the whole church? I once preached a sermon during the Week of Prayer for Christian Unity in which I suggested that all the English churches could and should claim the inheritance of Augustine's mission to Canterbury, and even the earlier spread of Christianity during the later Roman empire. At the back of the congregation one clergyman, whom I took to be an Anglican, shook his head vigorously. But the point seems to me to be both obvious and undeniable. Even those who divided from the Church of England, let alone that church itself in its separation from Rome, trace their roots to that original missionary activity.[15] The family tree does not have a simple genealogy – family trees rarely do; but if one is tracing the genealogy of mission the conclusion is inescapable. In this respect Protestants have done themselves significant harm in so often leaping from the early church (or even the New Testament) to the Reformation, thereby ignoring at least half, and sometimes three-quarters, of Christian history.

My point is more than historical. How do we claim that inheritance in practice? What importance do we attach to the signs of the continuity of the church through the ages? This is why the Bible and the sacraments, confessions of faith and the ministry of the church are important. We may differ in the relative importance we attach to each, but it is difficult to regard any of them as completely dispensable.[16] Indeed, sometimes those groups which have dispensed, to a greater or lesser extent, with one or more of these marks actually have their Christian identity sustained by their relationship with other Christian groups which have not gone so far. At the end of the 1970s, when discussions on a covenant among the English churches were taking place, I was invited to discuss them with the relevant committee of the Society of Friends. In the course of my remarks I pointed out that, although from one point of view they stood outside those discussions because of their position on the signs of continuity just mentioned, from another point of view their continued existence as a Christian group in England only made sense in the context of their relationship with the other Christian churches. Put another way, how would the Society of Friends maintain its Christian identity in the absence of other Christian churches? Would not its central affirmations either melt into, say, an Indian or an African religious environment, or alternatively require some more obvious emphasis on the kind of signs of Christian continuity which are so central in Faith and Order discussions?

The Society of Friends is not unique in this respect, but rather at one end of a spectrum. The same issue arises when non-episcopal churches gladly take note of statements made by bishops which capture the Christian mood of the moment, even though it is not "our bishop" who is speaking; it also arises when we appeal to statements of faith as criteria for right belief even though we rarely use them in worship. Perhaps we should say that there are not only signs of continuity, but a continuity of relationality, which needs to be acknowledged.

Continuity of relationality may help us better to understand the issues concerning particular theological or denominational traditions. Over the centuries particular Christian churches have developed certain characteristic "styles" of theological discussion and reflection. The patristic emphasis in Orthodoxy, the significance of justification among Lutherans, the emphasis on the sovereignty of God within the Reformed tradition are all illustrations of such styles. Is there a theological style characteristic of United churches, and is there a particular way in which United churches can relate to this diversity of theological style? This may seem almost an academic question, which does not impinge much on the everyday life of local churches. However, it does relate to the question of identity – certainly if anyone takes the position that a particular style of theological reflection is the only legitimate one, but also if it is argued that reluctance to choose between particular styles is a mark of an unsustainable eclecticism. A United church must aim at catholicity in its theology – a catholicity which is open to the whole of world Christianity.

How then should United churches relate to Christian world communions? This raises all the questions of identity which I have been discussing in this paper. When the United Reformed Church was formed in

1972, it decided that its primary ecumenical relationship outside Great Britain would be with the World Council of Churches rather than the World Alliance of Reformed Churches, and this was reflected in various practical ways in terms of finance and deployment of personnel. Over the years that position has been modified, and members of the United Reformed Church have since served the World Alliance both as Geneva-based staff and as officers and members of commissions. But the tension over whether we should give first emphasis to "United" or to "Reformed" in our name continues; and as little further progress towards organic union has been made, the number of those among us who wish to emphasize the essentially Reformed nature of our heritage has grown. I take the other position, but that is probably affected by my Churches of Christ background.[17]

Indeed, since 1981 the United Reformed Church has needed to relate to two Christian world communions; and other United churches may have to relate to more than two. Even though there are probably more United churches which are members of the World Alliance of Reformed Churches than any other Christian world communion, there are particular problems here. People of my generation still have a continuing memory of a time before union, and therefore can still identify with a non-United tradition. But for people in the United Reformed Church only ten years younger than me, that is more difficult; and for those who are younger it is more difficult still.

Apart from the German United churches and the United Church of Canada, most United churches have been formed since the second world war. The issue of the identity of United churches within Christian world communions is therefore only just becoming critical. Will members of United churches become increasingly marginal in the life of Christian world communions? And is the international life of Christian world communions becoming increasingly detached from the national lives of their member churches? Another possibility is that the nature of Christian world communions is changing as they cease to be dominated by North Americans and Europeans. The perception of the important issues which face the worldwide church is increasingly convergent, and it is not primarily determined by the particular theological and denominational traditions which led to the formation of the Christian world communions. In this context the greatest weakness of United churches may be their essentially national or sub-national nature.[18] United churches need to sustain their awareness of the world church; and the particular role of the World Council of Churches here may be more important for United churches than many others.

The identity of any United church may be focused in various ways: but ultimately what matters is the way in which it is able to sustain within its membership a sense of the ecumenical vision – a vision of wholeness and reconciliation within the whole inhabited earth. The identity of United churches cannot be less than the identity of the church as a whole – an identity which itself has something of the paradoxical contrast between two of St Paul's images from his letters to the church at Corinth: earthen vessels (2 Cor. 4:7) or God's building (1 Cor. 3:9, cf. 2 Cor. 5:1).

NOTES

[1] The theme of identity has been a recurrent one in consultations of United and Uniting churches: see notes from the second consultation (Limuru 1970), in *Midstream*, IX, 2-3, winter-spring 1970, pp.13-14; the report of the fourth consultation (Colombo 1981), section F, in *Growing towards Consensus and Commitment*, Faith and Order Paper no. 110, WCC, 1981, pp.16-18; and also the report of the sixth consultation (Ochos Rios 1995), §25, in *Built Together: The Present Vocation of United and Uniting Churches (Ephesians 2:22)*, Thomas F. Best ed., Faith and Order Paper no. 174, WCC, 1995, p.12, in which United and Uniting churches are called to redefine their identity in terms of God's mission and to reinterpret their history in the light of this.

[2] This is an over-simplification of a complex situation. The United churches formed in north and south-west Germany after 1817 "which forced Lutherans to acknowledge *de jure* the Reformed church [were] everywhere an act of state carried out by an enlightened generation of senior civil servants and law officers" (N. Hope, *German and Scandinavian Protestantism 1700-1918*, Oxford, Oxford UP, 1995, pp.321-22). However, whereas Frederick William III enforced this from the "top down" in Prussia in 1817, together with his own eclectic liturgical preferences, a church such as the Evangelical Church of the Palatinate, formed in 1818, was not only more evenly balanced between the two traditions but also more open liturgically and doctrinally. After 1866 constitutional changes giving greater self-government to the churches in the new North German confederation went hand in hand with assertion of the position of the king of Prussia as *summus episcopus*. The number of separate Landeskirchen was reduced in 1870, 1919 and 1945 as part of wider political changes. See Hope, *German and Scandinavian Protestantism*, pp.336-48,351-53,487-96.

[3] Bede, *Ecclesiastical History*, Book I, ch. xxx.

[4] A phrase most often associated with Hegel, who also termed it "the consummate religion": see G.W.F. Hegel, *Lectures on the Philosophy of Religion: The Lectures of 1827,* Peter C. Hodgson ed., translated by R.F. Brown, P.C. Hodgson and J. M. Steward, with the assistance of H.S. Harris, one-volume edition, Berkeley, Univ. of California Press, 1988, pp.391ff.

[5] *Ecclesiastical History*, Book I, ch. xxvi.

[6] Benedict Anderson, *Imagined Communities: Reflections on the Origin and Spread of Nationalism*, London, Verso, 1983; Ernest Gellner, *Nations and Nationalism*, Ithaca NY and London, Cornell UP, 1983; Gellner, *Nationalism*, London, Weidenfeld & Nicolson, 1997; Adrian Hastings, *The Construction of Nationhood: Ethnicity, Religion and Nationalism*, Cambridge, Cambridge UP, 1997.

[7] The root of this decision may be traced back to the encyclical letter of the ecumenical patriarch in 1920 when he proposed the formation of a "league of churches" – a fairly clear allusion to the newly formed League of Nations. The first draft constitution may be found in *Documents on Christian Unity: Third Series, 1930-1948*, G.K.A. Bell ed., London, Oxford UP, 1948, pp.292-97. Section V divided the membership of the WCC assembly and the central committee among regions, with special

provision for the Orthodox churches. The Lutheran world convention and the Baptist World Alliance had expressed a preference for the grouping to be on confessional rather than regional lines. This was discussed further at the request of the Lutherans between 1945 and 1947, and the constitution adopted by the first assembly of the WCC in 1948 abandoned the regional membership quotas and instead gave the assembly the responsibility for allocating seats on the central committee, and the central committee that for allocating seats in the assembly – "due regard being given to such factors as numerical size, adequate confessional representation and adequate geographical distribution": W.A. Visser 't Hooft, *The Genesis and Formation of the World Council of Churches*, WCC, 1987, pp.48-51,61-62; *Documents on Christian Unity: Fourth Series, 1948-57*, G.K.A. Bell ed., pp.202-203.

[8] For the sake of brevity I will refer simply to "United churches" from here on.

[9] The basis of union, after stating in §8 that the United Reformed Church "as a united church will take, wherever possible and with all speed, further steps towards the unity of all God's people", went on in §9 to state that the church "testifies to its faith, and orders its life according to this basis of union, believing it to embody the essential notes of the church catholic and reformed. The United Reformed Church nevertheless reserves its right and declares its readiness at any time, to alter, add to, modify or supersede this basis so that its life may accord more nearly with the mind of Christ." This is *both* an affirmation about its self-understanding at union *and* a commitment to be ready to change in the future.

[10] The Dutch case study, however, shows that this is not true in the Netherlands.

[11] "A uniting church discovers its own identity as it receives the heritage of various traditions and forms them into a diversity that is not simply 'reconciled' or 'comprehensive' but creatively integrated, a diversity which is able to learn from and incorporate a wide variety of traditions" (*Growing Towards Consensus and Commitment*, p.17).

[12] The birthday of the Scottish poet, Robert Burns, is celebrated with a special meal on 30 January. Occasionally some ministers have even used the local Caledonian (Scottish) club as a source for recruiting church members.

[13] See A.L. Macarthur, *Setting up Signs: Memories of an Ecumenical Pilgrim*, London, United Reformed Church, 1997, pp.104-106.

[14] E.g. C. Budden, "Questioning the Basis of Union", *Uniting Church Studies*, VI, 2, July 2000, pp.55-64.

[15] Those who trace their origins to Columba, or Aidan, or Ninian, also have to recognize that ultimately in the West all roads lead back to Rome, whatever route they took.

[16] The Toronto consultation pointed out that united churches "may be tempted to adopt an attitude of relativization and not to take seriously enough the continuity of the fundamental structure of the church...It is essential that united churches continue after union to struggle with questions of faith and order", *Midstream*, XIV, 4, Oct. 1975, p.546.

[17] See D.M. Thompson, "Reformed or United? Twenty-five Years of the United Reformed Church", *Journal of the United Reformed Church History Society*, VI, 2, May 1998, pp.131-44.

[18] "Organic union gives an opportunity to the churches to relate more effectively to the historical and cultural conditions of their country or area. United churches validate the universality of the church rather through their adaptability to cultures than through worldwide uniformity. They are, in principle, freer to address themselves to the vital issues of the society in which they live. They may be tempted to over-identify with that society. For this reason they need strong links beyond national boundaries" (report of the third consultation of United and Uniting churches, Toronto 1975, in *Midstream*, XIV, 4, Oct. 1975, p.546 – reaffirmed in *Growing Towards Consensus and Commitment*, p.22).

Churches Uniting in Christ

A Case Study in Identity

MICHAEL KINNAMON

Churches Uniting in Christ (CUIC), inaugurated in January 2002, is a covenantal relationship involving nine United States-based churches, including:

- the African Methodist Episcopal Church;
- the African Methodist Episcopal Zion Church;
- the Christian Church (Disciples of Christ);
- the Christian Methodist Episcopal Church;
- the Episcopal Church;
- the International Council of Community Churches;
- the Presbyterian Church (USA);
- the United Church of Christ;
- the United Methodist Church.

The combined official membership of these churches exceeds twenty-two million. Together with their two "partners in mission and dialogue" – the Evangelical Lutheran Church in America and the Moravian Church – they represent the "mainstream" of US Protestantism.

The roots of CUIC are in the Consultation on Church Union (COCU), through which Christian leaders laboured for forty years to realize some form of visible church unity. Several convictions expressed in COCU documents bear on our discussion of identity at this meeting.

First, COCU's initial plan of union reflected the ecumenical thinking about organic union prevalent when the Consultation was first proposed by Eugene Carson Blake in 1960. The model, that is to say, was one of structural consolidation, marked by common patterns of worship, a shared confession of faith, and a structure for making decisions together. The heritages of the uniting churches were to be honoured, but confessional labels subordinated in favour of a new common identity. This vision was, of course, set forth in classic fashion at the World Council of Churches (WCC) New Delhi assembly in 1961 and reflected in church unions throughout the 1960s, from Zambia to Jamaica, from Papua New Guinea and the Solomon Islands to North India.

Second, while attentive to the global ecumenical movement, COCU was also deeply and explicitly rooted in the United States context. In this way, COCU exemplified the insight expressed at its 1975 Toronto consultation: "United churches validate the universality of the church rather through their adaptability to cultures than through worldwide uniformity."

The US character of the effort can be seen in two ways. One is that the clearly stated purpose of the proposed union was to bring the gospel to bear more effectively on the problems of US society. For better or worse, the election of a Roman Catholic (John F. Kennedy) as president in 1960 probably increased the desire for a common Protestant voice in public life. Another is that COCU addressed not only the divisions associated with the European Reformation but also those associated with the key division in US society, namely race. The presence of three black Methodist churches ensured that divisions caused by white racism were always on the church union agenda – and, by the 1980s, central to it.

Third, COCU's vision from the outset was to manifest a unity that is "truly catholic, truly evangelical and truly reformed". It is important to remember that forty years ago these adjectives still conjured up images of warring traditions; they defined fundamentally different ways of being church. There were times when it would have been easier for the other participating churches to let the Presbyterians, or the Episcopalians, go their separate way (as they periodically threatened to do). The "identity" of the Consultation, however, demanded the presence of Reformed, Catholic and Evangelical partners – just as it demanded the presence of predominantly black and predominantly white churches. Without the participation of any one of these particularities, interest in COCU would surely have dried up altogether.

Fourth, leaders of the Consultation on Church Union intended for the envisioned united church to be a community of shared faith, as indicated by the extensive theological consensus document *The COCU Consensus*,[1] but with considerable room for continuing diversity of theology and practice. The section on baptism, for example, affirms that a diversity of baptismal practice points to different dimensions of the gospel (that is, God's initiative of grace *and* our response of faith) and should therefore not simply be allowed, but actually encouraged, in any future union.

* * *

The plan of structural union, sent to the churches for adoption in 1970, was not affirmed for several reasons (that appear more clearly in hindsight): a fear of losing legitimate diversity, including diversity of heritage; a fear of focusing on structure at a time of pressing mission needs, including civil rights and the US involvement in Vietnam; a sense that denominations were less the carriers of theological identity, and thus the source of division, than they had been even a decade earlier; a fear that union would actually open new divisions in the body of Christ; a plain old fear of change.

Instead of ending the Consultation, however, leaders began "living their way" towards a new ecumenical identity. This was a difficult period. Many church members, as well as the secular press, spoke of COCU's death. They had no conceptual alternative to what was often called "denominational merger" and, thus, assumed that the rejection of that model meant the end of the Consultation.

The new approach, parallelling similar developments in the wider ecumenical movement, emerged in the 1980s with the name "covenant communion". Elements of covenant communion were basically identical to what is generally known as "full communion": mutual recognition of each other as parts of the one church of Jesus Christ, mutual recognition that each confesses the same apostolic faith, mutual recognition of members in one baptism, regular celebration of the eucharist together, shared mission, and the mutual recognition and reconciliation of ordained ministry. "In covenant communion", according to the basic document,

> the churches may maintain, for so long as each may determine, their own structures and traditions, including present forms of worship, systems of ministerial selection, training and placement, their international, confessional, and communion relationships, and their mission programmes. What covenanting means is that these now separated churches will resolve to live as one in the most basic things – in faith, sacrament, ministry and mission. Uniformity in structure is not essential to covenant communion.[2]

The COCU Consensus had spoken of the mutual reconciliation of ministry on the basis of a common adoption of the historic threefold pattern with bishops in apostolic succession – a real stretch for at least four of the churches. The actual covenant proposal, however, suggested that these episcopal, presbyterial and deaconal ministries, whatever they may be called, can *already* be seen in the various churches – a shift that was highly problematic for Episcopalians. This impasse threatened the whole effort; and so a revised proposal, set forth by the COCU executive committee in 1999, asked the churches to bracket the question of ministry, reserving it for later intensive dialogue, while proceeding to inaugurate a new relationship, Churches Uniting in Christ, marked by the other elements of covenant communion. This proposal was subsequently approved by overwhelming majorities in all nine churches.

There are at least seven features of Churches Uniting in Christ (CUIC) which seem relevant to our discussion of identity.

First, for the past forty years the churches have related to an organization called COCU; now they must begin to relate more directly to one another. This is a question of identity that will make or break the entire effort. COCU was not an expression of church; it was a consultative body for helping to create the conditions for unity. CUIC is also not the church (each of the communions will continue to baptize and ordain as separate bodies), but it is much more a way of living as church together. It is a substantive covenant signifying that life together is an essential dimension of each church – less something they join than something they are. I must admit that the churches have, at best, only begun to make tangible this new identity; but it is a most important implication of their inaugurating promises.

Second, CUIC reflects the premise that not all issues of faith and order need be resolved before the participating churches can give formal expression to the life which, in many places and ways, they already share. William Temple put the matter this way in the letter inviting churches to become part of the WCC: "We may not pretend that the existing unity among Christians is greater than it in fact is; but we should act upon it so far as it is already a reality." Books on ecumenism sometimes speak of five "stages" of interchurch relations: competition, co-existence, cooperation, commitment and communion. CUIC can be understood as a movement from cooperation to commitment, on the way (though that sounds too linear) towards communion that will include a reconciled ministry.

This means, of course, that dialogue is an integral part of the new relationship, not just a prelude to it. CUIC should be seen within a complex web of relationships (Episcopalians and Lutherans, Reformed and Lutherans) that have dealt extensively with issues of ministry. Meanwhile CUIC has, itself, spawned new bilateral work: Episcopal-Presbyterian and Episcopal-Methodist. All of this, plus new partners at the table (this will be discussed below), holds promise for resolution of the issues at stake.

Third, the original proposal for covenant communion envisioned the establishment of "covenanting councils" in communities across the country as a way of holding the churches mutually accountable. The final CUIC proposal, however, eliminated any such prescribed structure. As a result, while CUIC has a national coordinating council and various working groups, it is less a structure than a framework for growth in relationships centred around sharing in sacraments and mission. It can be thought of as an officially sanctioned, mutual invitation for the churches to live differently with one another – especially at the congregational level. I expect the relationship to take quite different forms in different settings.

Fourth, COCU had already challenged the colour barrier in US Christianity more directly than any previous ecumenical effort. CUIC goes further, to make "combating white privilege" the mission core of the new relationship. It needs to be stressed that CUIC is not a social justice coalition; it is a sacrament-centred covenant. But combating racism is definitely seen as a key ecclesiological issue, as the acid test of the churches' commitment to live more closely with one another

Fifth, the CUIC proposal made clear that *The COCU Consensus* is foundational to the new relationship; but, in my judgment, a significant shift has taken place in the way this document is understood. Differences of theology and worship are now seen less as matters to be resolved through "consensus" than as gifts to be shared. If my students are any indication, there is little interest in common statements of doctrine or common liturgical practices, but considerable interest in learning from, and borrowing from, other traditions. The consensus text is appreciated by them to the extent that it enables such a sharing of gifts.

Sixth, as mentioned above, two churches have not joined the original nine under the category "partners in mission in dialogue" – which means, at a minimum, that they have made public witness with the CUIC churches in the struggle against racism and have become full participants in the dialogue on ministry. The image is one of concentric circles: full members of CUIC... partners in mission and dialogue... official observer-participants (e.g., the Roman Catholic Church)... the wider Christian family. This is a reminder that "uniting" is the operative word. The goal of this ecumenical effort, in the words of *The COCU Consensus*, is nothing less than "the unity of the universal church". The prayer is that CUIC will be a sign and foretaste of this goal.

Seventh, I used to lament that the 1970 plan of union was not approved, but I no longer do so. Had it succeeded, the churches might have been less likely to repent, more likely to glory in their institutional power. Besides, testing out different models is surely appropriate since no one model is a definitive expression of visible unity. So I prefer to confess that God has led us to this moment. But the dangers of the CUIC model are obvious: (1) that the relationship will be ignored since it does not involve the consolidation of structures, and (2) that the churches will sidestep the opportunity for genuine change. "Reconciled diversity", Lesslie Newbigin once wrote, "offers an invitation to reunion without repentance and without renewal, to a unity in which we are faced with no searching challenge to our existing faith and practice, but remain as we are."[3] A model of unity, if it is to deserve such a label, must be tangible enough to make a witness to the world, intense enough that those in it recognize their responsibility for one another, costly enough that churches are changed as a result of being in it, and intentional enough that the body of Christ is renewed through the sharing of gifts. It will be a generation before we know whether CUIC meets these tests.

One thing we can say for sure is that CUIC will affect church identity more quickly in some places than others. Already, some congregations are adding "A Member of Churches Uniting in Christ" to their signboards. Other congregations have yet to hear about the covenant.

If CUIC does take hold, then (as I see it) it will be a harbinger of the post-denominational church. Not an *un*denominational church, but a church that values the particularity of confessional heritages without absolutizing them; a church that sees identity in the sacramental and missional sharing of local congregations as well as through national, denominational structures for mission; a church that regards differences as intrinsically enriching rather than threatening; a church that vigorously challenges discrimination without undercutting the distinctive gifts of the African-American denominations. This would be a significant change of identity, indeed.

Author's addendum

Two years after the inauguration of Churches Uniting in Christ, the concern expressed in the seventh point above – about the dangers of the CUIC model – deserves reiteration. While CUIC is being enacted in some local settings, and while ecumenical offices in some churches have produced materials designed to raise awareness of CUIC, the national structures have, for the most part, ignored the existence of this covenantal relationship. The best prospect for new energy and attention is coming from the task force on the reconciliation of ministry which has produced a draft that will soon be presented to the churches for consideration. The recommendation that all of the churches adopt a threefold ministry with bishops in apostolic succession will surely "raise the ante" for involvement in CUIC!

NOTES

1 *The COCU Consensus*, Princeton, NJ, Consultation on Church Union, 1985, 1991.

2 *Churches in Covenant Communion: The Church of Christ Uniting*, Princeton, NJ, Consultation on Church Union, 1988/1989, rev. ed., 1995, p. 9.

3 "All in One Place or All of One Sort?", in *Creation, Christ and Culture: Studies in Honour of T.F. Torrance*, Richard W.A. McKinney ed., Edinburgh, T&T Clark, 1976, p.293.

A Case Study on Identity

The Communion of Churches in India

D. K. SAHU

The success of the church union movement in India is seen in the formation of the Church of South India and the Church of North India. A plausible explanation of the advent of ecumenism in India includes the mixture of two factors, the theological and the non-theological. In the context of the church union movement it was a question of identity and of relevance: the issue was not just a change from denominational identity to an ecumenical identity, but how to respond creatively in forming a new identity and being relevant in the social and religious situation of India.

The question of identity is important because there is a sense of foreignness attached to being Christian in India. The church has been trying its best to be Indian as well as Christian. One of the tasks of ecclesiology is to express the identity of a believing community, including helping the community deal with changes which inevitably come upon it. At the heart of the matter are two questions. The first is what gives distinctiveness to a community, recognizing that any group forms its identity by marking its boundaries. Once these boundaries are set up, the second question arises: How can they be sustained and justified? This in turn is necessary because the received notions of what it means to be a Christian may be called into question by the emergence of new circumstances or ideas, or by a new awareness and perspectives.

The story of founding a new community within the pluralistic Indian society is closely associated with the coming of modern mission. This community embraced a faith which arrived with a colonial power, and was dependent on finance from the West. It was made up of persons from various other religious communities and caste backgrounds, with the majority coming from lower castes and the economically backward classes; the challenge, therefore, was to integrate these different identities into one community. Sadly, in the course of history the visible Christian community in India, as elsewhere, has often failed to express the fruits of new life in Christ in a sense of renewal, freedom and dignity. Caste or class still persists in the Indian Christian community, in some form or other, and it is right to admit this more openly than has perhaps been done in the past.

Any serious consideration of the church as a new community must take into account the story of early Christianity in India: that is, the story of the Syrian Christians. There is no doubt that the history of Christianity in India goes back to an early period.[1] The nucleus of the Indian Christian community in the pre-16th-century period lay chiefly in what is now central Kerala, and this was unquestionably the first Christian community in India. The history of the Syrian Christians from the earliest times till the latter half of the 16th century was that of a single denomination. They were called Syrian Christians because of their relationship with the Eastern "Syrian" churches, and their liturgy in the Syrian language. In the following centuries the Syrian Christians were divided into three main groups: those who accepted the authority of the pope while retaining their Eastern rites and customs; those who recognized the leadership of the patriarch of Antioch; and the Mar Thoma Christians who were separated from the major group during the earlier part of the 19th century due to the impact of the Church Missionary Society.

A new chapter

The growth of 20th-century ecumenism is one aspect of the search for Christian identity. Even those who look on ecumenism with suspicion can scarcely fail to acknowledge that it has renewed the vision of the church. But the general impression might be that once a covenant is signed and the union consummated, uniting churches "live happily ever after". If this were true, then the story of some churches would have been different! However, the fact of coming together often causes tensions to be felt more severely than when the churches concerned were separate. The integration of actual local worshipping groups may prove more difficult than the unification of confessions, particularly when union is based on the principle of freedom of conscience.

The union of churches in India marked a transition from denominational identity to a corporate identity. But the question of ecclesial identity, when considered in a particular historical context like that of India, is not an isolated phenomenon. At any given time the church, as a particular expression of Christianity, is the outcome of an historical process of development and therefore takes differing forms in the course of history. Thus the uniting churches adopted the ideal of organic union as a contemporary expression of the identity of the church. This means that within the union, each uniting church was required to see its own identity as being not the whole, but rather a part of a larger, common identity. The strength of this new identity lies in the discovery of the richness of various traditions, along with the way in which groups of people in different regions make their own contribution to the witness and service of the church.

It is necessary for the church to "expropriate" – to express and live out – that which is intrinsic to its own identity as a *koinonia* (fellowship) in history. Therefore the church must be aware of the subtle ways in which the influence of certain factors can change its perspective and direction. In the context of India, the congregations are scattered over a vast country and live within a pluralistic society whose cultural milieu is thoroughly permeated by Hinduism. The self-understanding of the church, then, is influenced both by inherited Christian traditions and the socio-religious character of Indian society.

The goal is to inter-relate, in the corporate life and thought of United churches, both senses of identity: as an Indian and as a Christian. In the past, there have been several attempts to define the nature of the relationship between these two identities in the life and thought of Indian Christians. Theologians have spoken of adoption and adaptation of one or more features of the Hindu heritage for use in Christian theological reflection. Such adoption and adaptation would take the form of an "indigenization" or "contextualization" or "inculturation" of the Christian faith in the Indian context. These ideas are evidence of how complex and intricate a task it is to describe adequately the dynamic nature of an identity that must be Indian as well as Christian.

The model of union

It is difficult – and may be misleading – to divide union schemes into neat categories, but it is important to note the rationale by which each specific union plan is formulated, and especially its way of dealing with denominational differences. Each church union has a particular basis and rationale which, even when they are not clearly spelled out, is implicit in the procedures followed and formulas of union chosen. J.W. Winterhager gives a comparison of unions in Canada and South India, seeing the two movements as representing two radically different approaches to union. He regards the Canada project as the purest embodiment of the principle of Nathan Soderblom that union should come about through the fulfilment and enrichment of the various traditions. Then he characterizes the South India pattern as also based on dialogue, but emphasizing the *sacrifice* of traditional ways.[2] John Webster Grant objects to this analysis, saying that it has distorted both Canadian and South Indian history in order to provide "pure types" for easy identification.[3] A fairer way of stating the contrast might be to note that the Canadian union was largely inspired by considerations of life and work, while those who carried on the conversation in South India had to grapple with more difficult problems of faith and order.[4]

Generally the challenge in any scheme of union is continuing the efforts to evolve an indigenous and ecumenical church. A danger to the success of any scheme lies in the continued coexistence of denominational churches alongside the United church; this leads to ongoing tensions among all those concerned.

The two schemes of union in south and north India were almost parallel but the consummation in south India took place earlier than in the north. The Presbyterians were in the vanguard in the south India union movement. They had formed an All India Presbyterian Union in 1900, and in 1908 its south Indian section joined with the Congregational union to form the South India United Church. The Lutherans of the Basel Mission in Malabar joined with this church in 1919. Then the South India United Church, the South India Province of the Methodist Church and the four dioceses of the Church of India, Pakistan, Burma and Ceylon constituted the Church of South India (CSI) on 27 September 1947.

The inauguration of the CSI, and the achievement of India's independence in 1947, provided added incentive for the negotiators in the north to move forward. The vision was realized in the formation of the Church of North India (CNI) with the joyful reunion of six major denominations: the Church of India, Pakistan, Burma and Ceylon, the United Church of North India (an earlier merger of Presbyterian and Congregational churches), the Methodist Church (British and Australian Conference), the Church of the Brethren, the Disciples of Christ, and the churches connected with the Council of the Baptist Churches in Northern India.

A case study: the Communion of Churches in India

The genesis of the story of the Communion of Churches in India (CCI) goes back to the invitation by the CNI to form three commissions of representatives of the CNI, CSI and Mar Thoma Syrian Church of Malabar (MTC). Here the goal was to explore the ways and means of further cooperation and witness in India. This move was welcomed during the meeting of the CSI and MTC negotiation commission, held on 17 May 1974. The three churches appointed their representatives to the theological commissions of their respective churches, and these commissions began to function as a Joint Theological Commission (JTC).

The first meeting of the JTC was held in January 1975 at Madras. The object of the commission was further defined as exploring the possibilities of close cooperation between the CNI, the CSI and the MTC and discussing questions of faith and order and other relevant issues. The aim of this was that there might be union between these churches, keeping in mind the ultimate goal of all Christ's people in India: namely, the

fulfilment of the mission of the church. During its third meeting in September 1976, the JTC passed the proposal for a new model of union for these three churches; this was accepted, and the resulting Joint Council was inaugurated in July 1978 at Nagpur.

The late Russell Chandran, one of the active proponents of the Council from its formation, used to say that the Joint Council was established on the basis of the three churches acknowledging that they were already one church, because of their oneness in doctrine and the mutual recognition of their sacraments and ministries: the council was intended to give visible expression *to the unity which already existed*. One of the components of that visible unity was to be the adoption of a common name; but some saw a difficulty in this, fearing that to adopt a common name would mean the three churches losing their identities. In reaction to this, an organic unity which would include a common name was ruled out.

Thus the attempt was made to manifest oneness through a common structure, while retaining the autonomy of the three churches. According to the preamble of the new constitution, the object of the new structure is (1) to serve as the common organ of the member churches and of the whole church of Jesus Christ in India, (2) to help the churches to fulfil the mission of evangelization, (3) to strive with all people for justice and the integrity of creation, (4) to explore possibilities for common action for the fulfilment of mission, and (5) to consider questions of faith, worship and order as well as other relevant issues.[5]

In a joint meeting of the executive committees of the CNI, CSI and MTC, held 11-14 November 1999 at Charalkunnu, Kerala, it was unanimously suggested that the Joint Council be superseded by a new relationship with the name the Communion of Churches in India. This would reflect the growth in the actual experience of unity among the three churches. The suggested new name was adopted and recommended to the three churches for approval at a meeting held on 13-14 November 2000 at Calcutta. An official joint declaration and inauguration of this relationship is expected as soon as practicable [this occurred in March 2004 – ed.].

One major achievement of the worship and mission commission has been the preparation of a common calendar and lectionary, which is being well received. The commission looks forward to preparing a common liturgy. It is hoped that under the new name, and with an amended constitution, new avenues will open for a wider ecumenical unity and fellowship in India.

Conclusion

The question has been raised whether behind the ecumenical "verbiage" about unity the pursuit of church union is largely pragmatic, driven by practical considerations such as the need for more "efficient" organization and the like. Of course pragmatic considerations cannot be ruled out altogether. But the question of union needs to be addressed through the interpretation of the principle of unity in diversity, and the deeper issue of the identity of the uniting churches in relation to former denominational identities. Nor should we forget that the denominations themselves were also the outcome of the church's struggle for renewal.

The question of union demands wrestling with the realities of the church's task in a particular geographical context. The vast majority of Indians are Hindus and the majority of Christians in India are Dalits and Tribals. The inequalities and discriminatory practices found in Indian society are very much operative in the church as well. In such a situation it would be much easier for the church to cater to one particular type of social background. This might save the church from many painful strains, and be helpful in satisfying the particular religious interests of a certain group – but then the church could hardly stand up to proclaim the message that "God was in Christ reconciling the world to himself" (2 Cor. 5:19, RSV).

The very essence of the church is being a community of the people who proclaim themselves reconciled to God and to one another, through the life, death and resurrection of Jesus. Reconciliation in the church means *living out* together the reconciled life, and engaging in the mission of reconciliation in order to draw others into the fellowship of those already reconciled. It is God who reconciled the world to himself in Christ. It is easy to break away, but it takes ages to build up. Through all the misunderstandings, failures and ambiguities, our faith is that, in a very humble way, the Communion of Churches in India can continue helping transform narrow boundaries, setting up a sign of hope in the kingdom of God.

NOTES

[1] It is almost certain that there were well-established churches in parts of south India not later than the beginning of the 6th century C.E. and perhaps from a considerably earlier date. But it is probable that these were, at least in part, churches of foreigners, worshipping in Syriac and cared for by foreign priests and bishops. See Stephen C. Neill, *The History of Christianity in India: The Beginnings to AD 1707,* Cambridge, Cambridge UP, 1984, p.48.

[2] Jürgen Wilhelm Winterhager, *Kirchen-Unionen des Zwanzigsten Jahrhunderts*, Zürich-Frankfurt am Main, Gotthelf, 1961, pp.37-111 (Canada) and pp.112-224 (South India).

[3] Grant comments that issues of size, comprehensiveness and Canadianism were emphasized repeatedly in the discussion leading to the formation of the United Church in Canada on 10 June 1925 (despite the refusal of a substantial part of the Presbyterian church to enter it). It was the result of the interaction of a particular view of the mission of the church

with a particular national situation. The Canadian ideal was not to be a melting pot but a mosaic to which all would contribute their distinctive gifts. J. Webster Grant, *The Canadian Experience of Church Union,* London, Lutterworth, 1967, pp.23-24,36.

[4] *Ibid.*, p. 34.

[5] See "Minutes of the Joint Theological Commission of the CNI, CSI and Mar Thoma Syrian Church", 1975 and *passim*; *The Joint Council of the CNI, CSI and Malankar Mar Thoma Syrian Church: A Brief History and Interpretation*, J. Russell Chandran ed., ISPCK, Delhi, 1984; The Amended Constitution of the Joint Council of the CNI, CSI and MTC, 2001.

SUGGESTED READING

A.J. Appasamy, *Church Union: An Indian View*, Madras, CLS, 1930

J. Arrangaden, *Church Union in South India*, Bangalore, Basel Mission, 1947

S.Bayne ed., *Ceylon, North India and Pakistan*, London, SPCK, 1960

Lionel Caplan, "Class and Christianity in South India: Indigenous Response to Western Denominationalism", *Modern Asian Studies*, 14, 2, Oct. 1980, pp.645-71

Lionel Caplan, *Religion and Power*, Madras, CLS, 1989

"The Constitution of the Church of North India and Bye-Laws", Delhi, ISPCK, 1987

"The Constitution of the Church of South India", Madras, CLS, 1983

"Profile of A Christian Church: Report of the Evaluation Commission to Study the Life and Work of the CNI", Madras, Institute for Development Education, 1990

D.K. Sahu, *The Church of North India: A Historical and Systematic Theological Inquiry into an Ecumenical Ecclesiology*, Bern, Peter Lang, 1994

D.K. Sahu, *United and Uniting: A Story of the Church of North India*, Delhi, ISPCK, 2001

The Scheme of Church Union in Ceylon, Madras, CLS, 1949

Bengt Sundkler, *The Church of South India*, London, Lutterworth, 1965

M. Zechariah ed., *Ecumenism in India*, Delhi, ISPCK, 1980

III

Special Account

III

Special Account

The Dutch Reformed Church Family in South Africa

Lessons Learned on the Way to Reunification

PIET MEIRING

The church: made of paper?

George Bernard Shaw will not go down in history as the greatest theologian of the 20th century. To the contrary, he became one of the most outspoken critics of the Christian message and of the Christian church during his life-time. However, this does not mean that one should not pay attention to what he had to say. His estimation of the church, and the role the church was playing in society, needs to be taken seriously. While on holiday at Knysna, South Africa, at the beginning of 1932, the dramatist-philosopher, according to his own testimony, was inspired to write the story of a black girl who set out to find God. In *The Adventures of the Black Girl in Her Search for God* (1932) Shaw relates how the girl, deep in the heart of Africa, first heard of God. A lady missionary promised her that if she searched for God, she would find him – a promise which caused her to set out immediately on her adventure.

During her search she crossed mountains and seas, meeting not only various gods but also numerous saints, heroes, prophets and philosophers. One of the most remarkable of these was an ancient man with a long beard and old-fashioned clothes who balanced a peculiar structure, several stories high, on his shoulders. On closer inspection the old man turned out to be the Big Fisherman, Peter the apostle. The building on his shoulders, he explained, was an enormous cathedral.

> "Take care: it will break your poor old back," she cried, running to help him.
>
> "Not it," he replied cheerfully. "I am the rock on which this church is built."
>
> "But you are not a rock; and it is too heavy for you," she said, expecting every moment to see him crushed by its weight.
>
> "No fear," he said, grinning pleasantly at her. "It is made entirely of paper." And he danced past her, making all the bells in the cathedral tinkle merrily.
>
> Before he was out of sight several others, dressed in different costumes of black and white and all very carefully soaped and brushed, came along carrying smaller and mostly uglier paper churches. They all cried to her, "Do not believe the fisherman. Do not listen to those other fellows. Mine is the true church."

> At last she had to run aside into the forest to avoid them; for they began throwing stones at one another; and as their aim was almost as bad as if they were blind, the stones came flying all over the road. So she concluded that she would not find God to her taste among them.[1]

Shaw's story may in the first instance reflect his views of the church in England, or the way he came to experience Christians in his own country. But it also, uncomfortably, reflects the experience of the country he was touring when he was inspired to write his book. For in South Africa there would have been many contenders for the black girl's attention. In 2002 Christians in South Africa celebrated the arrival in Southern Africa of the Christian church – the Reformed faith – 350 years ago, which coincided with the landing of Dutch East Indian Company's commander Jan van Riebeeck and his party at Table Bay on 6 April 1652.[2] In the three and a half centuries that followed, millions of South Africans became followers of Christ. The church – the different denominations – grew and continued to grow, to the point where South Africa has become not only one of the most "Christian" countries in the world but sadly, also, one of the most divided Christian communities. Christians belonging to more than six thousand different denominations, following their leaders, are ready to throw stones at one another! The question may rightly be asked: How much weight does the church carry in the South African society? Or is it in the final analysis lightweight, constructed of paper?

The Dutch Reformed Church: first to arrive on the scene

The story I want to tell is of one about the South African churches, the first to arrive at the scene. The story of the Nederduitse Gereformeerde Kerk (the Dutch Reformed Church or DRC), as old as the story of the colonization of the Cape by Dutch settlers, is a story of faith and hope, of service, of sacrifice – but often, too, a story of failure and disobedience, of not living up to its calling, a tale of disunity, of heresy and of shame.

When Jan van Riebeeck landed at the Cape, his first official act on setting his feet on African soil was to read a prayer prepared for him by the Lords of Seventeen who were in charge of the Dutch East India Company (DEIC) in Amsterdam. The prayer, which was regularly repeated at the commencement of van Riebeeck's council, contained the petition for the local inhabitants that, through the establishment of a halfway station at the Cape,

> [we] shall conduce to the maintenance of justice, and the propagation and extension (if that be possible) of thy true Reformed and Christian religion among these wild and brutal men, to the praise and glory of thy name...[3]

True to his prayer, van Riebeeck and his successors did try to take care of the mission to the Khoi-San people in the area, as well as to the growing number of slaves that were brought to the Cape. Ministers, initially paid for by the DEIC, were encouraged to take responsibility for the spiritual well-being of all. Slowly but surely the church grew, among white as well as black. The Dutch Reformed Church was the only *religio licita* in the Cape: Holland had chosen for the Calvinist Reformation, and so would the colonies. The principle of *cujus regio, ejus religio* was accepted without question by one and all. The order of priority in van Riebeeck's prayer left no room for misunderstanding: "Thy true *Reformed* and *Christian* religion" was to be propagated! Those Hollanders who happened to be Lutheran just had to live with the fact that in the Cape they were regarded as being Reformed. It took almost a century and a half before the colonial masters softened their stance, allowing them to build the first Lutheran church in the Cape.

During the first 150 years a number of Dutch Reformed congregations were founded, not only in Cape Town and surrounding districts but also in far-off rural communities. Wherever the pioneer-farmers trekked, the church followed to provide for their spiritual needs. To the Dutch farmers the local churches became their bastions, not only of faith but also of culture and civilization, the institution that kept them together. At the same time the missionary endeavours at the Cape began to bear fruit. Since 1737, with the arrival of Georg Schmidt (the first full-time missionary to the Cape), and especially since the founding of the South African Missionary Society in 1799 (which facilitated the coming to South Africa of a number of missionaries from England and Holland), converts from the ranks of slaves, coloureds, and Khoi-San as well as the Xhosa joined the church.[4]

Unity tested – and lost

And then in 1806 the English, after one previous attempt, finally took control of the Cape. Gone were the special privileges of the Dutch colonists and farmers – and gone was the privileged position of the Dutch Reformed Church. The English governors threw the gates wide open and a host of new denominations made their way to the Cape: Anglicans, Methodists, Presbyterians, Congregationalists, Baptists, Roman Catholics. The farmers in the rural areas, especially, were caught up in a strange new world which they did not understand, and which they definitely did not appreciate. Having lost so much that was dear to them, they turned to the church, *their* church, to find solace and reassurance.[5]

In the next decades a series of events overtook the DRC which, looking back, provide textbook examples of how things can go wrong in a church, and of how a unity among believers which was once taken for granted was tragically lost.

Political upheaval

During the 1830s a large number of Dutch pioneers left the Cape Colony in protest against the English interference in their lives, and in order to find new homes in Natal, the Orange Free State and Transvaal. They were disgusted at the governor's policies, and angry at the accusations some missionaries (especially those employed by the London Missionary Society) levelled against them. They felt cheated out of their dues in the process of the emancipation of slaves. Above all, they wanted to be free, to live on their farms, ruled by leaders they had elected themselves in republics they could call their own. This, of course, brought the "Voortrekkers", as they called themselves, into conflict with the African tribes they met on their way, through whose land they trekked, with whom they bartered for land to build their farms. Bloody skirmishes as well as terrible battles were fought. As a result of all this, relationships between blacks and whites – also between black and white *Christians* in the Cape Colony, as well as in the Voortrekker Republics – were undeniably marred. The unity they had in Christ was sorely tested.

One church became three churches

No ordained minister of the DRC accompanied the Voortrekkers. This was partially because the church leadership was initially not overly enthusiastic about the Trek.[6] Also, the Cape church suffered from a chronic shortage of ordained ministers in the Colony itself. Pastors for the DRC were trained in Holland, and were slow in coming to South Africa. Many congregations in the Cape had to do without a permanent "dominee" (minister). In due course ministers were found for the Voortrekkers living in Natal and the Orange Free State, but the faithful in the Transvaal had to wait, seemingly in vain, for their own pastors. The government of the Zuid-Afrikaanse Republiek (Transvaal) wrote urgent letters to the church in the Netherlands, asking it to come to the rescue. Help eventually arrived in the 1850s, when two ministers from Holland volunteered; but their coming resulted in controversy and schism.

In 1834 a split had occurred in the Hervormde Kerk in Holland (the state church), when a substantial number of ministers and members left to found a new Gereformeerde Kerk which was to be less liberal in its teaching, and more orthodox in its liturgy and church order. It was evident that trouble was brewing when the first of the volunteers to South Africa, the Rev. Dirk van der Hoff, announced himself as having been ordained in the Hervormde Kerk; and the second dominee, Dirk Postma, was found to belong to the Gereformeerde Kerk. Van der Hoff organized the congregations he ministered to into a Nederduitsch Hervormde Kerk, whilst the congregations who favoured Postma's more conservative message formed a Gereformeerde Kerk. Soon afterwards the Rev. Frans Leon Cachet, sent from Natal by the DRC to straighten things out, arrived in the Transvaal to gather all congregations which did not feel at home with either van der Hoff or Postma back into the original fold of the Nederduitse Gereformeerde Kerk (DRC). The Voortrekkers, who had crossed the Vaal River into the Transvaal barely a decade earlier as members of one church, were now officially divided into three "sister churches". The division stands, even to this day.

Racism destroys the unity of the church

Then came the synod of 1857, when racism openly and ominously reared its head in the DRC. There were high hopes for the 1857 synod. The missions committee worked hard during the recess, preparing a proposal that would involve the DRC in foreign missions far across the borders of the Cape Colony. But synod, too, was confronted by a vexing problem: a growing racism in its midst. For a number of years, reflecting the changing political landscape as well as changing attitudes between white, coloured and black congregants, questions were raised about the necessity for believers from different groups to worship together and to share the communal cup. At the 1857 synod discussions came to a head when the presbytery of Stockenstrom presented the meeting with a *gravamen* asking synod for a ruling in this regard, since worshipping together and sharing communion together caused embarrassment among some.

After an exhaustive debate, synod accepted a compromise proposal by the Rev. Andrew Murray Sr (father of the famous Andrew Murray Jr), who was concerned that the debate would impact negatively on the proposals of the missions committee. The watershed decision that changed black-white relationships in the DRC for the next 150 years read,

> It is indeed desirable and biblically correct that our members from the ranks of the heathen should, wherever possible, be incorporated in existing congregations; but where this measure *as a result of the weakness of some members* would hamper the promotion of the cause of Christ, congregations built from the ranks of the heathens, or still to be built from these ranks, may enjoy its Christian privileges in a separate building or establishment.[7]

It is obvious that the synod adopted the decision mainly for pastoral reasons, and as a practical solution for a limited time. The concession proved nevertheless to be the thin edge of the wedge. Separate services became the rule rather than the exception, and eventually paved the way for separate synods, and finally separate denominations, to be formed along racial lines. In 1881 the Dutch Reformed Mission Church was established (for coloureds); in 1910 the first synod of the Dutch Reformed Church in Africa (for blacks in the Orange Free State) was constituted, followed by DRCA synods in the other provinces. The different regional synods were united in a DRCA general synod in 1962. Eventually, in 1968, the Reformed Church in Africa (for Indians) came into being. The pattern of apartheid had penetrated the church long before the term itself was coined.

For many years these developments did not seem to bother the Christian community too much. It fitted perfectly the 19th century Protestant missionary strategy formulated by the English missionary leader Henry Venn, together with his American counterpart Rufus Anderson,[8] which encouraged missionaries to establish indigenous national churches – self-governing, self-sustaining and self-propagating – among the different tribes and nations of the world. That is exactly what the Dutch Reformed Church family is about, propagandists would argue: we are one happy family, with different churches for different racial groups.

But the innocence was soon lost. During the early 1930s and 1940s the ideology of apartheid was gaining ground among Afrikaners. In 1948, after the National Party was voted into power, it became the official policy of government. South African society was slowly but relentlessly compartmentalized. Separate development with separate institutions for the different racial groups became the order of the day. For the majority of whites, the supporters and beneficiaries of apartheid, this indeed made sense: different churches for whites, blacks, coloureds and Indians. That many English-speaking churches did not follow suit, that some of their leaders strongly objected to apartheid, was considered irksome but understandable: they just did not grasp the grand scheme of things!

Voices of protest

Opposition to apartheid, especially against church apartheid, did not only come from English-speaking churches within the country. It arose from many quarters, from within South Africa as well as from abroad.

The "younger churches"

Albeit true that the different members of the DRC family seemed to live with the 1857 decision and the formation of the three "younger" churches for three-quarters of a century, a growing voice of protest was heard from the 1960s on. The disunity in the DRC family was questioned, and the cry went up: we need to become what we originally were, *one* church. I remember well the words of Ernest Buti, moderator of the general synod of the (black) DRCA, referring to the treatment the members of the so-called "daughter churches" received from the "mother church": "What kind of mother is this, that does not want her daughters back home, that does not welcome her children at the door?" Years later, Buti's son, Sam Buti, followed in his father's footsteps, since he was also elected moderator of the DRCA. His message was equally clear:

> We do not only want to be indigenous churches, we want to feel that we form part of the universal church of Christ. We want to be accepted as believers in Jesus Christ and not continuously classified as black/coloured/Asian Christians.[9]

In the ranks of the (coloured) Dutch Reformed Mission Church (DRMC), equally strong voices were heard. At its 1978 synod the message was unequivocal:

> The church wishes to express its conviction that the policy of apartheid and/or separate development upheld by the government is contrary to the gospel.[10]

Needless to say that these statements would lead to polarization within the DRC family, and that tension in the relationship with the so-called "mother church" arose from time to time. How deep the gulf, how bitter the resentment was, became evident at the meeting of the World Alliance of Reformed Churches (WARC) at Ottawa in 1982, when the three younger churches persuaded the WARC member churches to suspend the DRC – their "mother church" – from this Reformed world body because of its support of the policy of apartheid. That the young theologian Alan Boesak, a charismatic leader in the DRMC and a vehement opponent of apartheid, was elected president of the WARC created shock waves at home!

After Ottawa no one was left in any doubt as to the attitude of the black, coloured and Indian members of the DRC family. At the synod of the DRMC shortly after Ottawa, it was stated strongly,

> Because the secular gospel of apartheid is a serious threat to the testimony of reconciliation in Jesus Christ and the church of Jesus Christ, the N.G. Sendingkerk (DRMC) in South Africa declares that it presents the church with a *status confessionis* (that is, a matter on which it is impossible for believers to differ without coming into conflict with the testimony of the church). We declare apartheid or separate development to be a sin, that the moral and theological validation thereof makes a mockery of the gospel and that its sustained disobedience to the word of God is a theological heresy.[11]

Synod adopted the Belhar confession – a strong statement calling for an end to apartheid, the reunification of the DRC family, and a commitment from all Christians to the poor and marginalized in the country[12] – and set in motion the process that, in due course, led to the merging of the "coloured" and "black" sections of the DRC family through the constituting of the Uniting Reformed Church in Southern Africa (URCSA). The name was carefully chosen: the *Uniting* Reformed Church, to indicate that the process was open-ended and would be completed only when the white and Asian "family members" joined the fold.

The ecumenical community

Apartheid, and the DRC's defence of the ideology and practice of apartheid, also came under fire from the ranks of the ecumenical community, both outside and inside South Africa. The DRC was a founding member of the World Council of Churches, but in 1961 – after the WCC called the Cottesloe consultation together to discuss the worsening situation in the country in the wake of the Sharpeville massacre (1960) – the DRC severed its ties with the Christian world body. The critical voice coming from the consultation angered the DRC. As noted above, twenty-one years later the World Alliance suspended the DRC's membership because of apartheid (1982). Also at the regular meetings of another Reformed body, the Reformed Ecumenical Council, the DRC had to face the continuous criticisms of its member churches.

Within South Africa the same happened. The "Message to the People of South Africa" prepared by the South African Council of Churches (SACC) in 1961, in the wake of Cottesloe, contained a strong denunciation of apartheid in society as well as in the churches. That was but the first salvo. In years to follow the SACC continued to clash with government on apartheid issues, and continued to take the Afrikaans churches to task on these issues. It cost the SACC dearly. Many of their officials were banned or deported, others had their visas and residence permits cancelled. The SACC was investigated, and taken to court on a number of charges. Numerous church leaders were arrested. Finally, the headquarters of the SACC were bombed by the secret police. But the council, under the leadership of the likes of Desmond Tutu, Beyers Naudé and Frank Chikane, courageously kept up the struggle. On an individual level many of the local ecumenical leaders – including those in leadership in the Anglican, Presbyterian, Methodist, Lutheran and Roman Catholic churches –maintained good relationships with their DRC counterparts, but also, often relentlessly, kept urging them to let go of apartheid and to work towards unification in the DRC family.

I personally have the highest regard for these Christian leaders who never completely let go of their errant counterparts in the DRC, but continued to meet with them, to challenge them, and to encourage them on the way they needed to go. Most influential among them was Desmond Tutu, who often went out of his way to meet with DRC people – leaders, ministers fraternals, students' groups, journalists and editors – to help them look in the mirror, to try to make them understand the plight which millions of South Africans suffered, and to plead with them to break with apartheid and its evils. Many of his own colleagues did not admire Tutu for doing that. They would have preferred him to shun the DRC. But Tutu never gave up on the Afrikaner community – nor on the Dutch Reformed Church.

Voices from within the Dutch Reformed Church

Not everybody in the ranks of the DRC agreed with the official policy of the church; and through the years they made their voices heard as well. Sometimes these voices were strong and confident, at other times, in the face of much adversity, they were few and weak. As far back as 1948 when the National Party came into power and apartheid was adopted as future policy, two intrepid theologians, Bennie Keet and Ben Marais, warned against the DRC's stance and involvement. During the 1960s a younger generation of critics arose, among them Beyers Naudé and David Bosch who were willing to challenge the DRC from within – and who were willing to pay the price for their prophetic witness. In the early 1980s the minority voice in the DRC grew stronger. In 1981 a number of theologians teaching at the DRC faculties of theology at Stellenbosch and Pretoria published a *Reformation Day Witness*, calling for change. And in 1982 no less than 123 ordained ministers presented the church with an "Open Letter", charging the DRC to turn away from apartheid, and to heal the breach between the member churches of the DRC family. Needless to say, these critics of apartheid within the church would barely have survived without the encouragement and advice of their ecumenical counterparts, in South Africa as well as abroad.

"A sin and a heresy"

Eventually the DRC did come to the point where it changed its traditional stance on apartheid, confessing that the system was not only doomed to failure but that the theological argument behind it was no less than "a sin and a heresy". Time came when the church not only had to face its critics and the millions of South Africans who suffered the atrocities of apartheid over many years, but also had to ask forgiveness of its own membership, whom the church had let down. Over many decades the DRC, with the Bible in hand and with the confidence of its conviction, had provided a theological argument for apartheid, assuring congregants that apartheid was leading all South Africans to a fair and just dispensation, that separate development was in conformance with the will of God. And now, in shame and in penance, the highest body of the church had to confess "before God and man" that they were horribly wrong.

It took a long journey to arrive at this point. At the 1986 general synod the DRC began to question apartheid, warning against all forms of racism. The 1990 synod went further, calling racism a "serious sin", and committing the church to the process of reunification within the DRC family. This enabled Willie Jonker, an eminent DRC theologian, to declare to a rather startled audience at a church consultation at Rustenburg some weeks after synod closed down (November 1990),

> I confess before you and before the Lord, not only my own sin and guilt, and my personal responsibility for the political, social, economic and structural wrongs that have been done to many of you, and the results of which you and our whole country are still suffering from, but vicariously I also dare to do that in the name of the DRC of which I am a member, and for the Afrikaner people as a whole. I have the liberty to do just that, because the DRC at its latest synod had declared apartheid a sin and confessed its own guilt of negligence in not warning against it and not distancing itself from it long ago.[13]

The 1994 synod reiterated the church's resolve to turn away from the past, adding that the DRC also owed a heartfelt apology to the "prophets of the past" who warned against apartheid and were treated by the DRC "in an uncharitable and inappropriate way".[14] Ben Marais as well as Beyers Naudé appeared at synod and were welcomed back in the fold with joy. Again strong decisions were taken on the necessity for reunification of the DRC family.

Three years later, in November 1997, Freek Swanepoel, moderator of the general synod, appeared at the Truth and Reconciliation Commission's faith community hearing in East London, to reiterate the DRC's confession – and its commitment to the reunification of the DRC family.[15] In 1998, at the general synod, the final piece was put in place when the delegates, echoing the statement made by WARC eighteen years earlier, condemned apartheid as a "sin and a heresy". The church's confession was generally accepted by the ecumenical community inside and outside South Africa. Desmond Tutu, for many years the castigator as well as encourager of the DRC, spoke for many when he addressed Freek Swanepoel at the TRC hearing:

> I greatly appreciate what you are saying. It is difficult to confess and ask forgiveness... We have seen over the past years how the once rejected church has returned, confessed its guilt, admitted to the nation and its own members that it was in error, that thy have welcomed back their old prophets... I feel like telling the devil, "Just you watch it, the N.G. Kerk is coming!" It is wonderful having you with us. Healing has already begun.[16]

The "Madiba Jive"

The acid test of whether the DRC had really broken with apartheid is the progress made – or not made – in the process of reuniting the DRC family of churches. That has been clear to us for years, and discussions have been held on church unity within the DRC family over a long period of time. Already in the 1960s and 1970s meetings in this regard were organized between the coloured leaders in the DRMC and their black counterparts in the DRCA. In the early 1980s they commenced drafting a new church order, as well as one of the most important credal statements in recent history, the confession of Belhar, which was to serve as basis for the uniting process. It was a painstaking process, which from time to time ran into unexpected difficulties. But determination and good sense prevailed, and on a joyful day, 14 April 1994, the "coloured church" and the "black church" came together to form the Uniting Reformed Church in South Africa. The process of healing had begun!

Taking the next step, drawing the "white church" as well as the "Indian church" into the process, proved to be more difficult. It was not for want of decisions and resolutions; those were put on paper at every synodical meeting. The problem, however, was that there seemed to be a lack of dynamic follow-up after the synods closed down. Meetings were held on many levels, involving clergy as well as laity, but a lack of vision, lack of clarity on possible models for unity, strong differences in opinion on the necessity of the DRCA and the RCA also accepting the Belhar confession as one of their credal statements, as well as the absence of a proper timetable for the unification process – all this hampered progress. This frustrated and angered the younger churches. The frustration was compounded when, shortly after the formation of the Uniting church, a substantial number of ministers, with their congregations, broke ranks to reconstitute the old ("black") DRCA. A very painful period followed, with the URCSA and the DRCA taking one another to court to settle claims about church properties in many parts of the country. And the Uniting church keeps asking: How big a hand does the DRC – or at least individuals within the DRC – have in all of this?

"Have you noticed the way Nelson Mandela jives?" Daniel Maluleke – one of the leaders in the URCSA – asked me some time ago at one of our workshops. "His arms and his head, the top of his body sway to the music. But he has become old, and his legs are tired. His feet barely move. They stay put, in one place. That reminds me of our reunification process. A lot of music, a lot of movement to and fro. But our feet stays nailed to the floor!"

There are, however, signs of hope. In the Cape the leadership of the DRC family of churches called together a few months ago a "konvent", with representations from virtually all congregations, to recommit themselves once again to unity. A few weeks later the northern synods of the DRCA, the URCSA as well as from the DRCA followed suit. In October 2002 the DRC general synod will meet, among high hopes that decisions taken will help to bring the unification process to its conclusion.

Seven lessons

It has been my privilege for the past years to have been part of this process, attending most of the synods and meetings referred to in the paragraphs above. I have come to share the hopes and disappointments of my brothers and sisters in the DRC family. The seven lessons I have learned in the process, and which I review below, will no doubt be shared by many of them.

Racism dies slowly – if ever

The first lesson involves a painful admission. I have come to realize that racism dies slowly – if ever. To erase apartheid from the statute books of the country, from the policy documents of churches, was one thing; to erase apartheid from one's heart and mind, quite another. Very often, in my experience, the church union process slowed down because of a deep-seated racism still lingering in the hearts of congregants. Many arguments were used why the process was slow, many administrative difficulties quoted, but often it boiled down to white Christians who have become accustomed to their own structures and their own privileges, and who were unwilling or unable to reach out across the racial divide, to embrace and to share.

In a sense this had to be expected. In a community where apartheid reigned for decades, where racism was accepted as the norm, it may take generations to get it out of our systems. It may also take a special effort of black and coloured Christians to free themselves from antagonism and resentment, to trust completely a white hand offered to them. The Uniting church, too, is battling with similar problems. Colleagues in the URCSA often lament the fact that, while coloureds and blacks have committed themselves to one another, in some congregations racism and prejudice, overt as well as covert, are still hampering relationships. In

South Africa generally, in spite of meaningful progress made to build a democratic society, racism has not died. It flares up in many places – in sports arenas, in schools, in parliament, in the business community – and it surely, and tragically, impacts upon the Christian community.

It is far easier to break away than to reunite

A second lesson which is not learned easily from history is that while it is relatively easy to disrupt the unity and cause a schism in the church, it is very difficult, sometimes almost impossible, to reunite and to rebuild the church. Breaking takes but a moment; healing may take centuries. Leaders who sometimes, and for the flimsiest of reasons, leave the church to start their own, should think twice – and thrice – before doing that! The history of the DRC is a case in point. The breakaway from the Dutch Reformed Church of the two sister churches in the Transvaal, the Nederduitsch Hervormde Kerk (1853) and the Gereformeerde Kerk (1859), could – and should – have been prevented. It took but a few men at odds with one another to turn one denomination into three – and after so many years and after so many endeavours to bring the faithful together again, we are still apart. The same applies to the fateful 1857 decision by the Cape synod when, ironically around the sacrament of unity, because congregants did not want to share the communal cup, the unity was lost. It took *one* compromise-decision, at *one* session of synod, to disrupt the unity. And after a century and a half we are still battling to regain what we have lost.

In the process of reunification, who you are is more important than what you say

A third lesson is about living out one's convictions. It is true of individuals as well as of communities, especially of Christian denominations and congregations, that what you are is of far greater importance than what you say, than the statements you send out into the world. Modern communication theory tells us that the medium is the message. That has always been the case with the church – the strength of the early church as well as, often, the weakness of the church in centuries to follow. Love is the "body language" of the church, a language that speaks far louder than carefully crafted statements and synodical decisions. In the recent past, in the quest for the reunification of the DRC family there was no lack of words stating, and restating, the churches' commitment to one another.

But often the body language went missing: the reaching out for one another, the compassion, the carrying of one another's burdens. This also applies to individuals, to the leaders in the churches tasked to drive the unification process, as well as to the faithful in the pews. When they learn to love one another and trust one another, when they listen to one another, when they allow themselves to enjoy one another and have fun with one another, unity becomes a reality. But, sadly, this often is lacking, with most of the attention focused on policy positions, on settling vexing doctrinal and liturgical issues, on dotting the "i"s and crossing the "t"s, instead of on building up relationships between one another.

Reunification requires a two-way process

Lesson number four has to do with communication. As important as it is for the different churches involved in the process to keep their lines of communication open, is also necessary for the leadership to keep communicating with the local churches about the process – not only to challenge and to inform them, but also to consult and to be informed. Ideally, we need a well-directed top-down movement as well as an equally dynamic bottom-up movement towards unity. The history of the DRC family confirms the experience of many other churches in similar circumstances, that where local congregations were invited to participate in the process, urged to reach out to other local congregations, and share their own hopes and anxieties with one another and with their respective presbyteries and synods, the unification process has run smoothly. When local ministers, for whatever reasons, kept the process away from their congregants, not informing them properly and not urging them to become part of the process, there was little enthusiasm for – and even antagonism towards – unification.

In the Western Cape where the *moderamen* of the DRC regional synod went on a "road show" in recent months, meeting all the local churches and discussing all the ramifications of the unity process with them, the results were very positive. Other synods followed their example, reaping the same results. However, in synodical areas where this did not happen, attitudes on reunification were either indifferent or negative. The same applied to the URCSA. Local congregations that were prepared for the union over a period of time entered joyfully into the Uniting church. The fact that some congregations were not well prepared and were ill informed was quoted as one of the main reasons for the unfortunate break-away of a number of congregations, only months after the union, to reconstitute the "old" church (the DRCA).

Doing things together

A fifth lesson concerns common planning and doing. We discovered during the past years that doing things together is important. While some did the talking and organized workshops and consultations, others started working together to develop projects that could be undertaken jointly, and in the process developed new structures for cooperation on a permanent basis. Not only do we need one another in order to become effective witnesses in society and to address the physical and spiritual needs of our fellow South Africans; by doing so the DRC family members learn to love and respect, and trust, one another. One of the more hopeful signs that the churches in the DRC family are indeed beginning to bond are the many structures for cooperation put in place, on the levels of the local churches, presbyteries and regional synods as well as on the level of general synod, in order to coordinate the missionary and diaconal activities of the churches. Another area of cooperation is theological training. The URCSA in the Cape recently decided to join the DRC's faculty of theology at the university of Stellenbosch, and at the universities of Pretoria and the Free State (Bloemfontein) a growing number of theological students from the different churches are rubbing shoulders in class. This, it seems to me, is one of the best "investments" in the reunification process that can be made.

Distinguish between theological and non-theological issues

Lesson number six comes as no surprise to seasoned campaigners in the ecumenical arena. But we, in South Africa, had to learn the hard way that there are both theological and non-theological factors to contend with in the quest for unity. The theological issues usually seem the more serious, requiring our best attention. And indeed we have those: doctrinal differences, various interpretations of the church order that have developed over the years, and above all the question of how to handle the confession of Belhar which has become one of the dearest possessions of the URCSA, but about which some DRC ministers still seem to have reservations.

But in my experience the non-theological issues are the really dangerous ones. These are sometimes vague, and often escape a proper definition and analysis. But they are real, and involve many things: dealing with cultural sensitivities, language issues, lingering racism, remuneration, pension funds, the sharing of resources, to name but a few. I sometimes get the feeling that pastors and congregants who are not willing to face some of the more uncomfortable non-theological issues, thank their lucky stars for the theological issues, which they can discuss at length over a long period of time – thus providing an excuse for not addressing the burning non-theological issues as urgently and radically as they should.

Do not lose hope!

The seventh and last lesson is important: Do not lose hope. It is true to say that the ecumenical journey is not for the faint-hearted, that disappointments and setbacks are lurking around every corner. Men and women of courage and wisdom, with an unshakeable commitment to Christ and to his church, are needed, leaders and congregants with resilience who have discovered, along the way, the true meaning of faith and hope and charity. We need people who are able to see, behind the activities of men and women, and behind the processes of history, the hand of God at work, building and restoring his church in six continents. I once asked a well-loved South African pastor, years into retirement but still with a keen interest in church affairs, what his analysis of the South African situation was. Referring to the many denominations in the country, he sighed, "The situation reminds me of the prophet Ezekiel in the valley of the dry bones. All around me I see dead bodies, skeletons, the remains of a once mighty army." With a twinkle in his eye, he added, "But the Spirit is blowing from every direction. The bones are moving!" (Ezek. 37).

Not a paper church?

In my introduction I quoted George Bernard Shaw. His description of the church as made entirely of paper, of church leaders as inefficient old men, stone-throwing men with bad arguments and bad attitudes, makes one think. It cuts too close for comfort. May I, in ending my story of the Dutch Reformed Church family on its long and painful ecumenical journey, quote the words of an even greater man – also no theologian, but someone who has to be taken extremely seriously: Nelson Mandela. In 1994, just after his inauguration as head of state of the new democratic South Africa, President Mandela paid a surprise visit to the general synod of the DRC in Pretoria. He addressed the delegates in Afrikaans, not mincing his words about the atrocities of the country's apartheid past – and the involvement of the Afrikaans churches in this regard. "I am not saying this in order to rub salt into your wounds, because I am aware of the long struggle within the Dutch Reformed Church to eventually reject apartheid. I am conscious of the agonizing of many church members along the way." He then added that the real test, the acid test, of whether the DRC has really taken leave of apartheid would be passed the day the DRC family became *one* again. May that happen soon![17]

Nelson Mandela had it right. In the last analysis the question: Does the Dutch Reformed Church have any contribution to make, does its witness bear any weight in society?, should be responded to firmly by asking the second question: How far are we on our way to restoring the unity we once had? To most South Africans the establishment of one united Dutch Reformed Church in Southern Africa will indeed have great symbolic value. One of the historic bastions of apartheid will replaced with a new community of men and women from all racial groups praising God with one voice, loving one another with one heart. Such a church is not made of paper!

But we need to hurry. In five years time it will be 2007 AD, a full 150 years since the fateful decision that divided the church. Is it possible that when 2007 arrives, we will remember the day together in *one* united church? It seems possible – if we are serious about God's intent for the church, and about our calling in this regard. And if we allow the Spirit to move the bones!

Author's addendum

Scarcely one month after the consultation in Driebergen, the general synod of the DRC assembled in Pretoria (13-19 October 2002). Much time was devoted to the process of church unity. The moderators of the Uniting Reformed Church, the Dutch Reformed Church in Africa and the Reformed Church in Africa were invited to address synod. The following decisions were taken, virtually unanimously:

– that synod states its disappointment with the little progress made since the synod of 1994, when the DRC committed itself to the reunification of the DRC family;
– that synod mandates its executive general synodical commission to contact the other members of the DRC family urgently, to discuss the holding of a national "konvent", to prepare for the reunification of the churches;
– that local congregations as well as other church structures are urged to develop mutual projects, serving one another and serving the community;
– that a memorandum be prepared for the use in local churches on the need for unity, as well as on the praticalities of running projects together.[18]

In the wake of the DRC general synod, meetings ("konvente") between the different regional synods of the DRC, the URCSA and the RCA were held to re-enforce our commitment to unity, and to discuss the outstanding issues. Some of the standing committees of the three churches – especially in the fields of mission and charitable services – have merged, to help us develop one voice and one ministry. But we are not there yet. We are two years nearer to the deadline of 2007 – and much still has to be done. Pray with us that the Spirit will continue to move the bones!

NOTES

[1] G. Bernard Shaw, *The Adventures of the Black Girl in Her Search for God*, London, Constable, 1932, pp.30ff.

[2] G. Hofmeyr, *N G Kerk 350,* Wellington, Lux Verbi BM, 2002, pp.28ff.
[3] *Journal of Van Riebeeck*, 8 April 1652, English transl. Du Plessis. See J. Du Plessis, *A History of Christian Missions in South Africa,* London, Longmans, Green, 1911, p.23.
[4] J. W. Hofmeyr and Gerald J. Pillay, *A History of Christianity in South Africa,* Vol. 1, Pretoria, HAUM, 1994, pp.40ff.
[5] David Bosch, "Racism and Revolution: A Response of the Christians in South Africa", in *Occasional Bulletin of Missionary Research*, 3, 1, 1979, p.13.
[6] Hofmeyr and Pillay, *A History of Christianity in South Africa,* pp.96ff.
[7] Nederduitse Gereformeerde Kerk (DRC), *Acta Synodi*, Cape Town, DRC, 1857, p.171 (my italics).
[8] J.J. Kritzinger, P.G.J. Meiring and Willem Saayman, *On Being Witnesses*, Halfway House, Orion, 1994, pp.8ff.
[9] F.E. o'B Geldenhuys, *In die Stroomversnellings,* Kaapstad, Tafelberg, 1982, p.24.
[10] Nederduitse Gereformeerde Sendingkerk (DRMC), *Handelinge van die Sinode*, Kaapstad, DRMC, 1978, pp.399,559.
[11] Nederduitse Gereformeerde Sendingkerk (DRMC), *Handelinge van die Sinode*, Kaapstad, DRMC, 1982, p.3.
[12] G. D. Cloete and D.J. Smit, *'n Oomblik van Waarheid,* Cape Town, Tafelberg, 1982, pp.14ff.
[13] Flip Du Toit *et. al.*, *Moeisame pad na Verandering*, Bloemfontein, Barnabas, 2002, p.106.
[14] Nederduitse Gereformeerde Kerk (DRC), *Handelinge van die Algemene Sinode,* Pretoria, DRC, 1994, p.374.
[15] Piet Meiring, *A Chronicle of the Truth Commission*, Vanderbijlpark, Carpe Diem, 1999, p.279.
[16] *Ibid.*, pp.277ff.
[17] My transl.; cf. Nederduitse Gereformeerde Kerk (DRC), *Handelinge van die Algemene Sinode,* Pretoria, DRC, 1994, p.536.
[18] *Die Kerkbode*, 1 Nov. 2002, p.4.

FURTHER READING

David J. Bosch *et al.*, *Perspektief op die Ope Brief,* Kaapstad, Human en Rousseau, 1982

John W. De Gruchy, *The Church Struggle in South Africa,* Cape Town, David Philip, 1979

Piet Meiring, "The Churches' Contribution to Change in South Africa", in *Change in South Africa*, D.J. van Vuuren *et al.* eds, Durban/Pretoria, Butterworths, 1983

IV

Bible Studies

Unity, Mission, Identity

In Paul's Ephesus – and Now?

JET DEN HOLLANDER

Scene 1: Driebergen, the Netherlands – 2002 AD

Lord, we are searching,
all of us, everywhere
for life in its bare essentials: food, health, shelter, peace;
for life that's worth living: love, happiness, community, meaning.
Lord, we long for life in all its fullness.
At times we look for it in the wrong places
and pursue it in the wrong ways.
So we return, time and again, to your word,
trusting that in entering the stories of your people long ago
we, like them, will find light on our path
and your hand to guide us in the right direction.

Scene 2: "Babel" – BC/AD

Reading of Genesis 11:1-9, with three voices (the narrator, the people, God).

Scene 3: Ephesus – about 55 AD

Content: An imaginary reading of Paul's considerations when writing his first letter to the Corinthians.

Setting: Paul is starting to write his first letter to the Corinthians (actually his second, but we do not have access to the first). He is in Ephesus, around 55-56AD, on his third missionary journey. Paul seems to have received complaints from Chloe (orally), but also a letter from the church leaders. He begins with the greetings but soon gets stuck. He decides, after some hesitation, to telephone Apollos to discuss the matter, as Apollos also knows Corinth (having gone there from Ephesus, and apparently having had a quite successful ministry there).

Paul: *(Thinks: the year of our Lord 55; reads aloud what he is writing)*

- From Paul, called by the will of God to be an apostle of Christ Jesus, and our brother Sosthenes,
- To the church of God at Corinth and so on,

- Grace to you and peace from God our Father and the Lord Jesus Christ.

(Stops writing, thinks out loud) But what next? How to tackle the issues they raise, and their quarrelling in Corinth? This is going to take some diplomacy. Or should I speak plainly? After all, it was I who taught them, and I know something of their weaknesses. On the other hand, I can't deny that their situation is particular, and difficult. I wish I could talk with someone who knows them too. Of course there's Apollos, it's not all that long ago that he was in Corinth...

But no, I don't really feel like consulting him. He's so *Greek*, and so popular there – well, he can't help that, but it's also because of him that the Corinthians are making all these comparisons, wanting to attach themselves to this leader or that! And why they had to become so critical of me, I really don't understand. It's not as if I'm doing this kind of work for my own salvation, is it? It was for *theirs*. Actually, I had better not forget that the point now is to help them to understand their calling. And Apollos did seem to communicate well with them, let me see... *(dials Apollos's mobile phone number)*

Apollos: *(switches on his mobile)* Peace be to you, Apollos here!

Paul: Apollos, brother, peace be to you as well. This is Paul, your brother in the Lord and fellow apostle, still residing with the church in Ephesus.

Apollos: Brother Paul, what a surprise to hear your voice! You are still in Ephesus, you say? How are our sisters and brothers there? And how are my beloved parents in the faith doing, for whose teaching I still give thanks to God everyday?

Paul: As for Aquila and Priscilla who nurtured you in the faith, yes, they are fine. They still speak of you regularly, and with great fondness and respect for what you did, first here in Ephesus and then in Corinth, for which they helped you prepare.

And as for the church, well, we too are feeling the effects of the recession, you know. There's a riot in the air, with the reduced trade because of the harbour, and now the silversmiths are feeling threatened by our preaching of the Way. People are looking for scapegoats and one of these days their anger will erupt.

But anyway, that's not what I'm calling about. It's about the believers in Corinth really. Apparently there are a lot of internal quarrels going on there.

Apollos: Yes, I heard something about that too, and it doesn't surprise me. They are such a mixed group of believers, with such a variety of backgrounds, interests, gifts and passions, aren't they...

Paul: Exactly, and so I got two passionate messages, one by word of mouth from Chloe's people and also a written one from the leaders, raising all kinds of questions. And in truth, I cannot blame them for being confused; at times I wonder too how to make sense of all the memories and stories about Jesus passed on to us in the past twenty years, and what it really is that God has shown us in him. I mean, much of it goes against our common sense, and then of course in Corinth you have all these philosophers and mystery religions promoting a totally different outlook on life.

Apollos: But don't forget, it's only four years since you began to teach there, and notwithstanding their quarrels they have really grown tremendously, both in faith and in numbers.

Paul: That's true, and... *(somewhat reluctantly)* well, it's happened not least because of what you did there. You watered, so to speak, the seeds that I had planted, and many came to faith.

Apollos: Well, yes, I must say that I very much enjoyed my time there. The church was very responsive, something really clicked between us. Perhaps it was because I myself had only just begun to understand what baptism in Christ means – and of course they love some good rhetoric.

Paul: *(sarcastically)* Yes, I heard about your powers of oratory there. Well, that's what I tried to avoid. I didn't want to seduce them with plausible words of wisdom, but convince them with a demonstration of the Spirit and of power.

But the problem is: how to respond to their questions in words they can understand. Take their endless quarrels. How to show them that they are one in Christ, notwithstanding their very real differences?

Apollos: Well, perhaps indeed by using words they understand. I always thought you had a gift for using familiar concepts to make your own point. So talk to them in terms of things they all know: they have great architecture, so talk of buildings; they love the Isthmic Games, so talk of sport; they are part of the Roman commonwealth, so use that idea. And, well, they are seduced by wisdom cults and so on, so deal with that; but they also have bodies... so use that image too. Do you intend to write to them soon?

Paul: Yes, I've already started a letter. In fact, I meant to have gone there already, but I've been delayed so I had better finish this letter quickly... Well, Apollos, it has been good to talk with you – surprisingly, really, because we two are so different. But I must admit, you have sparked off some ideas! Let me develop them further... and I may even send you a copy of the letter by courrier.

Apollos: I look forward to it. My love be with you. *(both switch off their mobile phone, and Paul goes back to thinking out loud)*

Paul: Now where was I? Right, I had this greeting... Then I'll first say some encouraging words... and then probably I should begin with Chloe's point, about the dissensions, let's see now... *(He writes)*

Reading of 1 Corinthians 1:10-17

Paul: *(thinks out loud)* Right, this clarifies at least to some extent how I understand my calling, and the need to maintain the unity of the Spirit. Still, tomorrow I need to put in something about Apollos' point... huh, these Greeks, always so interested in the body, but I must admit it's an excellent image – the church as a body with many parts! I wonder if I also shouldn't use it in my letter to the Romans! Anyway, that's for later. So, something about being a body with different parts and each with a task to fulfil; something about running a race perhaps, and then something more on Christ crucified, because there is a link there with their misunderstanding about baptism, and the one who baptized them. Ai, how they are struggling to be faithful... I pray that the Spirit may give them light, and me too. *(Paul freezes)*

Scene 4: Driebergen – 2002 AD

From Babel and Ephesus back to Driebergen

So here we are, back in Driebergen with our questions of unity, mission and identity. How do they relate and belong together? And most importantly, to what kind of unity and mission and identity are we called today? These are large questions which are at the heart of many ecumenical discussions today, be it in the World Council of Churches, the Lutheran World Federation, the World Alliance of Reformed Churches, or regional bodies like the Conference of European Churches or the All Africa Council of Churches.

They are also at the heart of the Mission in Unity (MIU) Project for which I work, and the MIU experience is probably the same as yours: there are no easy answers. The Mission in Unity Project was set up in 1999 by the World Alliance of Reformed Churches and the John Knox International Reformed Centre because the Reformed family had become increasingly aware that it is very divided and that, in many cases, this is not enhancing the credibility and effectiveness of our mission.

Unity and mission are closely related, even if there are no simple equations like "united efforts = relevant mission", while "divisions = non-effective mission". Of course the reality is more complex than that. But that the considerable degree of competition, non-cooperation, isolation, division and quarrelling in the Reformed family – escalating at times to the point that different factions of one church beat each other into the hospital – does not enhance our witness, is beyond doubt. Hence the creation of the MIU Project as a deliberate effort of the Reformed family to continue its analysis of mission and unity in their inter-relation, and also to facilitate initiatives of churches which search for new expressions of mission in unity.

The name of the project is significant: Mission in Unity. Unity and mission are two sides of one coin, but the name places mission first, to indicate that the ultimate aim of the project is to assist the churches in being authentic witnesses to Christ. Within that framework the focus is on the question of whether unity will enhance our witness. Is it a matter of working towards union, or actively engaging in cooperation – and with whom? This quest often involves a number of key questions:

- How do we understand mission (and first of all, *God's* mission?)
- How do we understand our part in God's mission (cf. 1 Cor. 3, being God's fellow workers), while acknowledging that we are not God's only partners?
- Who do we think are God's partners? Who are our partners? Do God's partners and ours overlap?

In summary: what is God doing, what are we called to do, and with whom should we be working together, in one way or another, in today's world?

Our context today

There are many ways to characterize our context today, but we might agree that one key characteristic of the present world is conflict. If nothing else, our arrival here on 11 September 2002 has reminded us of the global conflicts that led to last year's horror in New York and the "war on terror" that has followed it. At all levels our world is full of conflict and fragmentation. How to interpret this?

Recently the missiologist Christopher Duraisingh identified two opposite forces at work in the world today.[1] On the one hand there is a centrifugal force of alienation and fragmentation, described already in the archetypal story of Cain and Abel. Cain can develop his identity only in terms of what he is not, in binary opposition to what his "other", Abel, is. He constructs his "other" as an enemy to be silenced and eliminated. Recent history shows the terrifying extremes to which such conflicting and exclusivist identities can lead: ethnic cleansing in the former Yugoslavia and Rwanda, or Osama Bin Laden's Jihad versus George W. Bush's War on Terror.

In Corinth too, as everywhere where human beings interact, there is a hint of these dynamics. As highlighted by Walter J. Hollenweger in his famous play *Conflict in Corinth*,[2] the Corinthian church seems to have included a group of well-to-do citizens such as Erastus and Gaius, who apparently weren't all that happy with the ways in which Chloe's people (including slaves and dock workers) wished to express their faith, speak in tongues, and have women speak publicly in meetings. The strategies then might not have been very different from ours today: to discredit the messenger in order to discredit the message, to think up rules why their opinions should not be heard, ways by which you ensure that their ways of being no longer disturb you. In short, in Corinth too there may well have been something of the centrifugal force of alienation and fragmentation, conflict and warfare that is so present with us today.

At the same time there is, Duraisingh suggests, an opposite force at play, the centripetal force of assimilation and homogenization. It is the attempt to tame and manage the plural particulars, to destroy differences and integrate all into a single world-view, as typified in the story of Babel with its desire for just *one* story, one language, one truth, one religion: "Come, let us make a name for ourselves; let's unite and be strong!" But that, according to the biblical writers, is not in line with God's intention. So God too, ironically, says: "Come, let us go down and confuse them." Human beings have a strong desire for sameness, a desire to recreate others in our own image so they will be familiar to us. Something of this desire for uniformity can be seen in the drive for Christendom, with its uniform (by whose standard?) "Christian" values, and the internationalization of Islam; but also, of course, in the dynamics of the global economy and the "McDonaldization" of societies.

Duraisingh notes that ultimately both the centripetal and the centrifugal forces lead to exclusion, fragmentation and conflict. This is so because even the tendency to make everything uniform and the same calls up resistance and a renewed search for particular identities, for holding on to what distinguishes you. The problem is that this may be pursued in an exclusivist and destructive way.

If this reading of (at least some dynamics of) the contemporary situation is valid, what does this mean in our world of unprecedented plurality, a plurality with which almost everybody, everywhere, is nowadays constantly confronted? What is needed? What should be key elements of mission today? Duraisingh's analysis is comprehensive in this respect too; and I cannot do justice to it here. But two of his points may be noted.

The first is the need to learn to live constructively with differences. Instead of seeing the "other" – the one who is different from me – either as someone who must become just like me or as an enemy to be ignored or destroyed, we must learn to take the other seriously as "other", as one whose differences complement me and through whom I become authentically myself.

The second is the need for reconciliation as a central paradigm for mission today. This emphasizes that in order to move beyond fragmentation and conflict, a central aspect of the church's mission should be our witnessing to a God who brings into being a reconciled human community, reconciled across all that divides us from God, from one another and from creation. In other words, thinking about mission begins from an eschatological starting point rather than a distinction between "us" within the church and "them" outside it. The vision of humanity which, in all its diversity, is being reconciled to God in Christ opens the way to acknowledging the "other" as a fellow traveller on the way to that new future. This is to think in terms of partners complementing each other and thus needing each other to move forward towards the vision of reconciliation in Christ.

Affirming differences as complementary

Returning to our Bible readings, we may conclude that on the one hand, we should not go the "Babel" way: trying to become strong by forming one uniform power bloc. On the other hand, we should also not go the "Cain and Abel" way or, in a mild form, the Corinth way: desiring to eliminate the differences, not accepting alternative ways, threatening division, withdrawing into exclusivism. The question is: Can we find a third way? Can we develop ways of unity and community which acknowledge differences and otherness, and which do not ignore or try to eliminate the otherness of the other, but affirm it as an essential prerequisite for becoming what, and who, we are meant to become ourselves?

Most of us have already experienced the fact that others add something to ourselves; that it is through them that we become who God intended us to be: I need you, and you need me, however difficult that sometimes may be to accept. Voltaire once said, when you disagree with me, you enrich me. To what extent do we experience our differences in this way? Does the otherness of others indeed enrich us, or does it rather frighten or enrage us? There is some evidence to suggest that in the church too often the latter is the case, probably because we are poorly trained in appreciating differences.

Group study: questions for consideration

Assuming that in an increasingly pluralistic world it is indeed essential to learn to deal constructively with "otherness", how might this apply concretely to different areas of church life? It may be worthwhile to look at three areas which are presently on the agenda of the Mission in Unity project, as they are likely to be on the agendas of many of our churches.

1. In the North, where demographic changes of recent decades have generated a new awareness of plurality, a major "mission in unity" challenge is that of possible cooperation between immigrant churches and mainline churches. The case study presented at this consultation by Francis Amenu ("The Ghanaian Ministry for London: A Case Study on Unity") highlights some of the missiological and ecclesiological challenges involved. How is your church presently addressing these issues?

2. How does your church seek to cooperate with other churches within your country? Are you involved in unity processes? Who are the partners? Which churches are not approached for closer cooperation? How do we deal with the otherness of others in terms of doctrines, involvement in society, styles of leadership, church order, liturgy? What did it cost Paul to work in partnership with others, and what is it costing us?

3. The same questions can be applied to theological education. Do our theological colleges acknowledge the approaches and emphases of other colleges in the country? Do we compete with or tolerate one another, or do we actively seek interaction with other colleges in the awareness that the other's approach might complement our own? In what spirit are the future church leaders being nurtured? Are there limits to cooperation?

Each discussion group is asked to bring back a short intercessory prayer on the discussion topic; this will be brought into our closing prayers.

Author's addendum

Questions of identity are at the heart of our divided world and church today. Since our meeting in 2002 it has become even clearer how much these questions need addressing, but also how difficult they are. Mission in unity involves more than mere collaboration. The challenge is nothing less than rethinking the nature and calling of the church and the churches, recognizing "unity" as God's gift, searching for ways to give this unity visible expression, and being changed in interaction with others.

But in doing so, what elements in our identity do we need to retain, and what do we need to let go? Which boundaries need crossing, and which ones need respecting? The increasing plurality of the globalized world often frightens churches into closed identities. But it also signifies a kairos moment for learning unity in diversity by practising it. As the United Protestant Church in Belgium recently said about the multicultural ministries which are developing here and there: "It hasn't been easy or painless. More like an 'if the grain doesn't die' experience. But like the grain, our church life is being renewed, we are rethinking our mission, and we are attracting people who for many years did not find a home in the church."

May God give us wisdom to distinguish between the boundaries to respect and those to cross – and the courage to cross the latter as we journey on towards one reconciled humanity.

NOTES

[1] In "Mission towards Reconciled and Intercontextual Communities", *International Review of Mission*, XCI, 363, Oct. 2002, pp.483-99. This paper was originally presented at a consultation in London, England, 14-19 April 2002, convened by the World Council of Churches' Commission on World Mission and Evangelism (CWME) and involving the Community of Churches in Mission (CEVAA), the Council for World Mission (CWM) and the United Evangelical Mission (UEM).

[2] See *Conflict in Corinth, and Memoirs of an Old Man. Two Stories that Illuminate the Way the Bible Came to be Written*, New York, Paulist, 1982.

Approaching Identity through Exile

A Welsh Perspective

PETER CRUCHLEY-JONES

Given our overall theme, I wondered what sort of "demonstration of power" we might expect from the Spirit – not least we in Wales, with our tradition of church growth through revival (despite our experience of decline). Paul, understandably, feels that the stirrings of a new community of faith represent exactly this phenomenon. But does it still do so today?

Lino Pontebon:
The Angry Christ.

I wanted to gather, in addition to Paul, some other biblical traditions about the work and power of the Spirit. These encounters with the Spirit remind us of C.S. Lewis's comment that humanity's search for God is like a mouse's search for a cat. Consider, for example, the Philippino artist Lino Pontebon's picture of the angry Christ. This picture emerges from the artist's identification with the workers' rights movement, and powerfully captures the sense of passion and challenge that Christ brings. Will we assume that Christ brings any less passion and challenge to us as Western churches? Through the insight and experience of some Welsh churches I wish to invite us into a difficult, contested, even painful place, which is set out for us in the biblical passages I am dealing with.

"People of God"? – Paul, with a subtext from Hosea[1]

Now remember what you were, my brothers and sisters, when God
called you
When the Lord first spoke to Israel through Hosea,
he said to Hosea, "Go and
from the human point of view few of you were wise or powerful
or of high social standing
get married; your wife will be unfaithful,
and your children will be just like her"
God purposely chose what the world considers nonsense
in order to shame the wise
So Hosea married Gomer. After the birth of their first child,
a son, the Lord said to Hosea
and he chose what the world considers weak
in order to shame the powerful.
name him "Jezreel", because it will not be long
before I punish the king for the murders
He chose what the world looks down on and despises,
and thinks is nothing
committed at Jezreel. At the valley of Jezreel
I will destroy Israel's military power.
in order to destroy what the world thinks is important.
Gomer had a second child, the Lord said name her "Unloved"
because I will no longer
This means no one can boast in God's presence.
But God has brought you into union
show love to the people or forgive them. After Gomer had weaned her
with Christ Jesus, and God has made Christ to be our wisdom.
By him we are put right
daughter, she became pregnant again and had another son.
The Lord said to Hosea name him
with God, we become God's people and are set free.
"Not my People", because you are not my people and I am not your God.

These are two readings that characterize the paradox and dissonance now facing many Western Christians, the dissonance at the heart of our identity today. People of God – or not people of God? We would like to preserve the Pauline confidence in who we are; yet we feel keenly Hosea's subversion of that confidence. In our ecclesiology and liturgy we make grand claims for the church's importance to God; yet our daily lives witness to the redundancy of the church in society. Our ecclesiological and liturgical statements describe and reflect a world that no longer exists; yet some of us still long for it. I want to illustrate further this dissonant contrast with two pictures that capture the iconography of our condition.

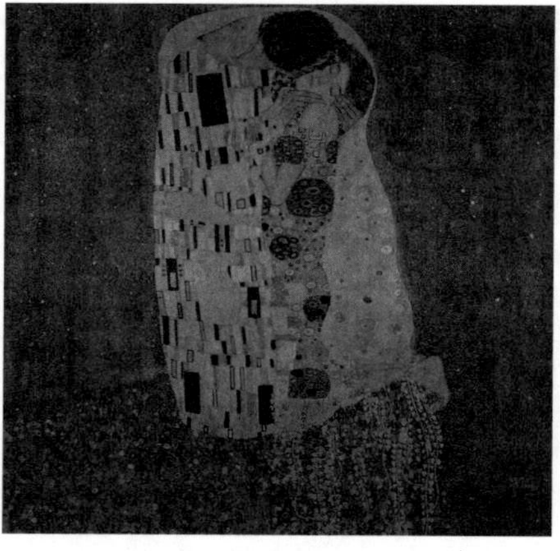

Gustav Klimt: *The Kiss* Österreichische Galerie Belvedere Vienna. Used by permission.

Firstly, "The Kiss" by Gustav Klimt. It is a picture of two figures enfolded in each other. It is radiant with light, with gold, it shines with the golden moment of the beloved's kiss. It represents the Pauline adoption of the church into the heart of God, our fond sense that we, who were far off, have now been brought near and have this special place at the side of God. And then secondly, "The Scream" by Edvard Munch. In this picture we find a figure running, emitting one long, silent scream against a distorted and nightmarish backdrop. It represents Hosea and the sense that our cherished theology is in chaos, it is distorting and breaking down. We are no longer at the side of God, no longer enfolded in his golden kiss.

Edvard Munsch: *The Scream* National Museum of Art, Oslo, Norway.

An exilic paradigm

In our experience of decline and displacement as a faith and as a church in the United Kingdom, I have been led by the congregations I serve in Wales to explore and offer the exile from the Hebrew scriptures as our biblical experience of today's realities. These congregations felt under threat, felt that the community they were trying to serve did not notice them or care for them. One woman commented to me, "It used to be that everyone went to church, now you're the odd one out if you go." This deep sense of disorientation and loss has made us inward-looking and fearful. It has made us feel that our identity is somewhere between that of victims and traitors: victims of social change we cannot control any longer, and traitors to a God who expects that we should be big, powerful, domineering churches as in the old days. And in all this we have to live with the uncomfortable thought that God has grown strange to us.

The breakthrough into this exilic paradigm came as a result of an elderly lady's comment: "The world is a terrible place – it was much better during the war." Through this comment we recognized our shared sense of crisis in theology, mission and identity. These sentiments were tied up with being unable to identify where God was outside the church – and what's the value of his being only in the church, if the church is dying? The sentiments were also the product of wanting to kick out at our community and world for ignoring us. One man even told me, "They'll be sorry when we've gone."

So the biblical exile has become an important story for me, but I need to make three preliminary remarks about this.

Firstly, as we come to consider our identity and mission in exile we must be careful that we do not simply respond like the writer of Psalm 137, with its mixture of nostalgia, depression, sanctimony and ill-suppressed vindictiveness: the hermeneutic of suspicion needs to be applied to ourselves! Needless to say, we have not been as careful here as we should have been. "Gospel and culture" statements are full of aggravated antagonistic anti-world polemic. "Western culture is inimical to the gospel," says Lesslie Newbigin. Meanwhile I want to believe in the God *of* history rather than the God *in* history and I desperately hope that God is *beyond* the church, because it seems to me that history is in the hands of culture rather than the church.

Secondly, it makes no sense to me from the UK experience to claim that the identity of God's people is fixed, static and assured through baptism, eucharist or ministry. The extent to which we are "God's people" depends entirely on the extent to which we are involved in God's mission. Will he tell us, "I never knew you"? The question is a real one. For, it seems to me, the church is *not* pre-eminent in God's plan; indeed God's experiment with the church in Western life – if it was ever God's experiment – may well now be over. If the church did not exist, mission would still take place. This is how much our institutional flesh is "like grass".

Thirdly, I wonder if we can be trusted to move from unity to mission when our identity is so rooted in ecclesiology – which, combined with liturgy, is the real home of the Western church's self-deception. In other areas of our thinking in the Western church, be it mission or theology, we have increasingly jettisoned the imperial God for the crucified God, but not in ecclesiology or liturgy. In these areas we still bathe ourselves in reflected glory, deluding ourselves that "God rules the joint" and that we are God's lieutenants left to "run the place" in his absence.

The meaning of exile

Our Zion is in ecclesiology. But the biblical exile saw the overrunning of Zion, first in its northern kingdom and then in its southern kingdom, by the geo-political ambitions of its superpower neighbours, Assyria and then Babylon. In those powerful social and political forces, however, Israel saw the hand and boot of God. The loss of king and of temple pointed to the end of the covenant, and provoked a profound reappraisal of Israel's life, politics and history. It is also provoked a profound reappraisal of God, who had grown strange to Israel.

But so grievous was the exile experience, and so subversive of the official ideology of an elect people, that the exilic stories take up a powerfully contested place in scripture, as the "people of God" wonder: Why did it happen? Who is to blame? How can we get at them? What should we do now? Where is Yahweh? Who is Yahweh? What is Israel for? Who belongs now? When can we go back to the way things were before?

A great deal of effort was spent trying to bolster the ideology of an elect, even if it had to be applied to an ever-smaller group. And, sadly, it is most evident at what we presume to have been the "restoration" of the "people of God", when the rebuilt temple walls offered the platform for Ezra to impose an ethnic purity that Joshua would have been proud of. It also provides the platform for the dismantling of whatever society had been created by those not taken into exile, by the poor who had remained in the land after the fall of Jerusalem. For Ezra sought not just the restoration of the ecclesiological rule of the old order, but also the restoration of its allied social and political rule. (And meanwhile: no one notices the Babylonian influences on the story of Genesis!)

How do we approach our story?

As we in the congregations worked with these exile stories we had to decide for whom and against whom we were reading them. This was necessary because different possibilities of reading were open to us. We could swallow the whole exile experience with an anti-Jewish attitude ("they are a stiff-necked people"); or we could read with a Welsh non-conformist, anti-priest attitude ("well, what do you expect from a faith for which everything was guaranteed by the temple and its priests?"). In either case we continually read ourselves into the role of the "good guy", the ones in the position of privilege.

We might also swallow the exile story as that of a minority who must seek ever higher walls behind which to hide, a minority which must drive a greater and greater wedge between itself and the contemporary world, doing so safe in the knowledge that *we* have the light, the truth, and one day *they* will realize it. Here separation is the only way to cope with plurality, the only way to protect our identity, especially separation from those "call-themselves-Christians" who believe in dialogue – or from those "call-themselves-Christians" who don't, for there is plenty of intolerance all around. But once again, we were in the "good guy" role.

We might abandon ship, reducing the identity and purpose of the church simply to internal matters such as liturgy or ecclesiology. We might pursue a sacramental ministry that somehow seems sufficient within the sanctuary alone, with no need to look beyond it. We might tell ourselves that all God wants is our worship. We might kid ourselves that when Jesus said, "Do this in memory of me", he meant, "Share a meal that originally even included Judas the traitor – and now excludes women from its presidency (*sic*) and the sister churches' faithful from its elements." (Do we really think that on that last night, all of Jesus' ethical and missionary life was summed up and reduced to a liturgical mandate, a mandate we have gone on to honour mostly by squabbling amongst ourselves?)

I want and need the comfort of the text, but is that only my own self-interest speaking? Looking into the eyes of Pontebon's angry Christ, I think that our identity is not so comfortable or so settled. So questioning ourselves as the "good guys", learning to read the story *against* ourselves, came from the realization that the exile represented God's embracement of Babylon, the apparent stranger, and his rejection of the apparent favourite, Israel. Israel sought to represent the exile as the rejection of particular elements of Israel, such as the kings or the idolators. But as the prophets showed, it was in fact *all* of Israel's life that God rejected, for it had all lost touch with the real life of God's people, with justice. True, the temple and king had especially lost touch with this life: this life which Israel's liturgists and ecclesiologists insisted was so fulfilling and authentic, was already lost from God. Might this be true of us, as we are seeing a similar demonstration "of the Spirit and of power"?

Life in the exile

In our context in Wales, that meant to me God's embracement of the plural culture of Western life and God's rejection of the desire for white mono-cultural Christianity. It meant God's rejection of "church" as the satisfaction of certain liturgical and ecclesiological urges. It meant the whole reappraisal of church being a force in the land, wanting power and prestige, practising again the imperial sanction and having the total truth. Newbigin, in his favouring of gospel over culture, of church over world, suddenly didn't look so bright.

So I want to turn now to a dramatization of aspects of Ezekiel for some clues to the identity and mission of those sent by "a demonstration of the Spirit and of power"... into exile. I hope it will show, like Hosea, how subversive God is, and how painful it is for a priest like Ezekiel to identify himself with this dreadful thing which God was doing by leaving Zion.

The detention of Ezekiel

Introduction

We find ourselves in the Babylonian headquarters of Israel's Religious Police, looking into interview room 1. (It may be a trick of the one-way glass – or the work of the Spirit.)

The scene begins with two religious police officers (RP1 and RP2), one of whom has a large file of papers and an empty chair.

RP1: Let's just review the case against our next client.

RP2: *(looking at file, reading and thinking aloud)* "Mortal man, do you see the disgusting things the people are doing here, driving me farther and farther from my holy place..." lalala... "The dazzling light of the Lord's presence rose up..." lalala... "and moved to the entrance of the temple,..." lalala... "The living creatures began to fly, and the dazzling light of the presence of the God of Israel was over them. Then the dazzling light left the city and moved to the mountain east of it."[2]

RP1: Right, bring him in. *(Ezekiel is brought in)*

RP1: You are Ezekiel? *(looks at his papers)* Ezekiel... the prophet?

Ezekiel: That is what the Lord our God has called me to be.

RP2: Ahhh, "the Lord our God has called" you...? I think *we* will be the judge of that.

RP1: You were a priest in Jerusalem? In the temple?

Ezekiel: *(remains silent)*

RP2: *(consults his files)* In fact you have served since the reign of King Josiah *(pauses to look at Ezekiel)*. You don't need to keep quiet, you know; we know everything about you.

Ezekiel: Then you don't need to ask me any questions.

RP1: Aren't you ashamed then?

Ezekiel: *(remains silent)*

RP2: *(voice rising)* Aren't you ashamed? For all these years you have been fed by the temple, housed by the temple, honoured by the temple. Do you think you are greater than Solomon? Do you think you know the mind of God? Do you think the Lord our God would turn his back on his covenant promise? Would God leave his temple?

Ezekiel: *(remains silent)*

RP1: We are a chosen people, a royal priesthood, his Spirit rests on us! Us! Not you, you misguided fool. You have abandoned our faith, you who once taught it. We are in a time of national emergency, don't you see how dangerous is this talk of God abandoning the temple? This is not the time for controversial and unorthodox theologies.

RP2: There will be no dissent, our people need leadership, guidance, certainty, they must cherish the past and the old ways, the true ways. How can they live in Babylon if they think the Lord our God has abandoned the temple itself? If that's true, then what is there to return to? What can we look forward to? Are we no different from all the other nations? You would sweep away all that is holy, all that makes us who we are!

Ezekiel: *(gathers himself to speak)* The Lord spoke to me and said: I will make Samaria and all her villages prosperous again. Yes, I will make you prosperous too! You will be ashamed of yourself, and your disgrace will show your sisters how well off they are.

Didn't you joke about Sodom in those days when you were proud, and before the evil you did had been exposed?

Now you are just like her, a joke to the Edomites, the Philistines, and your other neighbours who hate you. You must suffer for the obscene, disgusting things you have done. I will treat you as you deserve, because you ignored your promises and broke the covenant. But, I will honour the covenant I made with you when you were young, and I will make a covenant that will last forever. I will forgive all the wrongs you have done, but you will remember them and be too ashamed to open your mouth. The Sovereign Lord has spoken.[3] *(pause as the police officers look in anger at him)*

RP1: Take this man and throw him out. We have no room for his sort. *(Ezekiel is taken away)*

We read Ezekiel 12:1-7, in which Ezekiel becomes a refugee.

Will the Spirit sustain a self-important church?

This imagined drama of Ezekiel speculates about the experience Ezekiel must have gone through and the cost to him personally as he, a priest, tells us that God has walked out of the temple, shaking the sand from his feet. He too inhabited the terrible space between the Kiss and the Scream. Jeremiah had told them from the very door of the temple that this would happen: do not believe, he said, in those deceptive words, "This is the Lord's temple, this is the Lord's temple, this is the Lord's temple." In our readings of this story my churches and I had to ask, "Could God do that again?" If we say we are in exile then is God with us, in the way we've always told ourselves and others that he is?

I have to consider the possibility that God is no longer an ecclesiological proposition or if, indeed, he is any longer an ecclesiological reality. From a mouse's search for a cat, it has become a mouse's search for cheese, and now we are trapped. Has *God* become a refugee from the Western church?

Consider what it would be like if 1 Corinthians 1:26-30 were re-expressed in such a subversive and exilic mode, so that the power of the Spirit confronted – rather than confirmed – our ecclesiology. It might go like this:

Now remember what you were, my brothers and sisters, when God called you
From the human point of view
few of you were wise or powerful or of high social standing
God purposely chose what the *church* considers nonsense
in order to shame the wise
And he chose what the *church* considers weak in order to shame the powerful.
He chose what the *church* looks down on and despises, and thinks is nothing
In order to destroy what the *church* thinks is important.
This means no one can boast in God's presence.
But God has brought you into union with Christ Jesus,
and God has made Christ to be our wisdom. By him we are put right
With God, we become God's people and are set free.

I have come to think that what we consider "exile", God considers "restoration"; and what we consider "restoration" is to push God back into exile. In our previous Bible study, Jet den Hollander introduced the Tower of Babel story in Genesis 11. Might we see the pluralizing of humanity in this story as God's response to the aggressive monoculture of Babel? Similarly, the exile sees the plurality of God's world and life restored as Israel must admit Babylon's place in God's world-view. But we are not to forget that with this plurality comes the clear demand from the prophets that we respond to God in the pursuit for justice, and not the pursuit for... ecclesiology.

Stanley Spencer: *Christ in the Wilderness: Scorpion*
 Collection, Art Gallery of Western Australia.

I want to add a final picture: Stanley Spencer's temptation of Jesus. Here Jesus sits on a rock cupping a scorpion in his hand. It captures a despairing, even suicidal air. The exile stories make us face the impact we have on God: that we both make room for God, and push God out. This dynamic transience of God is not honoured in our ecclesiology or liturgy, which makes God settled and sure; yet it is the creative principle in mission. It is the factor that makes it *God's* mission, and thus makes mission something that is always changing and emerging, growing and failing in relation to us and our context. But as we face up to this transience in God, are we only to say that God has abandoned Western life and culture? Perhaps we should now take refuge from the church – like Ezekiel. Perhaps we are now being freed from the church as it has been.

But it is difficult to be freed from a comfortable imprisonment. I remember a Jamaican story about a man who is in the country and comes across a farm. In the field the farmer has chained a John Crow (a vulture) to a post, so that the vulture flies in circles around the post keeping the crows away. The man thinks this is wrong; he goes and breaks the chain in order to free the bird. Well, some time later he passes this way again and there is the John Crow and the broken chain – but the John Crow is still flying in circles above the farmer's field. For as the Reggae singer Bob Marley has told us from Jamaica: free yourselves from mental slavery, none but ourselves can free our minds.[4]

The plurality in Western life asks of us questions about justice, peace and community that might lead us into new partnerships, not unlike that of Cyrus and Yahweh. It might even lead us into new forms of theology, just like Israel who came to shape its scriptures out of its exposure to Babylonian stories and themes. But it might not rebuild the church.

So Ezekiel offers us an "antidote" to Western self-referential faith and identity. The antidote in these passages is twofold. Firstly, the embracing of the refugees' life and perspective thoroughly subverts our self-satisfied sense of our place in God's eternal plan. Our identity and mission is to be carved out away from the supposed safety of the sanctuary; it prompts the renewed search for a home that still has not been found anywhere other than the place where we live. This also means a spirituality rooted in a vulnerability which ecclesiology and liturgy have rarely practised in the West.

Secondly, it invites us to identify with the ethics and righteousness of God over and against the traditions of the church. This is to call us back into a search for justice, and a siding with the struggle for life over death. It calls us also into the role of story-tellers, telling again God's story of life out of death and being re-configured through those stories. But above all it is to call us into mission and away from ecclesiology. For it leads us to see that exile is experience of being sent and thus a missionary experience, one whose aim is not that we return to where we started but that we serve where we are, in the midst of an uncertain world – which God certainly loves.

Finally I want us to listen to this song in the spiritual, *A Motherless Child,* sung by Paul Robeson. It sounds the voice of the refugee, the truly abused minority whose humanity has been denied. I've chosen it to say that this is *not* the church's voice. However much the church grieves its loss, we have lost nothing worth keeping if we have been *sent* into exile. Instead I suggest we listen to it and hear God singing, singing to us, out of his exile experience of a church whose ecclesiological obsessions have excluded him. Let us listen to the song with the prayer, "Let plurality roll":

> Sometimes I feel like a motherless child
> Sometimes I feel like a motherless child
> Sometimes I feel like a motherless child
> A long ways from home.
> A long ways from home.

A long ways from home.
A long ways from home.

Sometimes I feel like I'm almost gone
Sometimes I feel like I'm almost gone
Sometimes I feel like I'm almost gone
A long ways from home.
A long ways from home.
A long ways from home.
A long ways from home.

Because my mouth is wide with laughter
And my throat is deep with song
You do not think I suffer
After I have held my pain so long
Because my mouth is wide with laughter
You do not hear my inner cry
Because my feet are gay with dancing
You do not know I die?

Paul Robeson

Questions for discussion

1. Would Ezekiel walk out of your church or join it? Could you imagine life without ecclesiology?
2. What are the comments of churches and Christians outside of the West about the identity of the Western churches as they see it?
3. What biblical stories seem to tell the story of your own church and context?

NOTES

[1] Based on 1 Corinthians 1: 26-30 and Hosea 1:1–9.
[2] Extracts from Ezekiel 8, 10, 11.
[3] Cf. Ezekiel 16:53ff.
[4] See Bob Marley's "Redemption Song" from the album *Uprising*, Bob Marley Music/Blue Mountain Music Ltd., P 1980, Islands Records Inc.

"What Kind of Fools Are We?"
God's Wisdom in Our World Today

BERTRICE Y. WOOD

In this Bible study on 1 Corinthians 1:1-2:16,[1] I wanted to invite the representatives of United and Uniting churches and church partnerships to consider ways of moving boldly towards embracing the unity that is ours in Jesus Christ. Each of our churches brings to the ecumenical community certain traditions and practices which are precious and central to our own understandings of faith and ecclesiology. Yet I sense that at times we are unwisely protective, unwilling to abandon ourselves for the sake of the unity of Christ's church. How do we regain our will for church unity, that passion reflected in the vision and commitments of those who have led us, in the past, into our United and Uniting churches? Are we willing to examine ourselves, and our churches, about the obstacles we encounter in bringing to fruition our endeavours to live into the unity that Christ gives? If held up to the test, do we truly consider that our union processes and relationships are gifts from God, rather than our own creations? Are our decisions truly responsive to God's guidance? And is inability to move forward reflective of a failure to be open to God's leading?

Context revisited

Let us consider one of the primary concerns expressed in Paul's letter known as First Corinthians. Paul writes from Ephesus about his deep concern over the news he has received that there are serious divisions within the church in Corinth:

> Now I appeal to you, brothers and sisters, by the name of our Lord Jesus Christ, that all of you be in agreement and that there be no divisions among you, but that you be united in the same mind and the same purpose. For it has been reported to me by Chloe's people that there are quarrels among you, my brothers and sisters (1:10-11).

He then elaborates on the connection of these quarrels to the mistaken practice of identifying oneself through baptismal affiliation with particular leaders, rather than through an understanding of belonging to the undivided community of all the baptized.

For Paul the scandal of disunity is serious; it is tantamount to dividing up Christ. And so at this particularly tense time in the life of the early church, when the nascent Christian community is developing its understanding of the faith and of Christian community living, Paul wants to address forcefully any misconceptions about what it means to be part of the church.

It is important to note that, while Paul was speaking to a problem manifested in the situation in Corinth, he suggests that the failure to embody the unity of the church is not something to which only that community may fall prey. Consider that in the salutation Paul indicates he is writing "To the church of God that is in Corinth… together with all those who in every place call on the name of our Lord Jesus Christ…" (1: 2). We might today speak in terms of the "local" and the "global" considerations of the call to live as one community of the baptized.

On wisdom and foolishness

Paul writes both to encourage and to chasten the church. He acknowledges with gratitude the spiritual gifts manifest in the community, and thanks God that the church in Corinth is not lacking in the spiritual gifts necessary for its sustenance (1:4-9).

Then, however, after reporting the news that he has received from Chloe's people, he proceeds to speak to them about God's wisdom, contrasting this with the foolishness of those who do not know the power of God. We note that Paul contrasts the situation of those "who do not understand the cross" with those who are inside the church, being saved. Yet might we not ask how much *we*, even as those within the community of faith, still fail to understand fully the power of the cross? Are there not ways in which we retain some of the character of those for whom the message of the cross is foolishness? And might not some, or even much, of our frustration or our hesitation to commit ourselves courageously to the unity of the church, be signs of what was apparent in Corinth? Could it be true that our own identification is, in many ways, based on baptismal affiliation with certain leaders or traditions, rather than with the undivided community of the baptized?

Let us not forget that we seek to live into the unity that God gives, so that we might witness in the world to that unity. These concerns are related to the mission of the church to manifest God's intentions for transforming the world. In Churches Uniting in Christ, in the United States, we have committed ourselves to work towards the mutual recognition and mutual reconciliation of our member communions' ministries, and towards the eradication of racism. We know that to do one of these without doing the other misses the opportunity and mandate to live into a unity that embraces the fullness of God's unifying love and justice as revealed in the ministry, death and resurrection of Jesus the Christ.

Because of our ecumenical relationships in local, national and global contexts, we are increasingly aware of the impact of the scandal of division on the urgent needs for justice and reconciliation in the world. Gratefully, ecumenical encounters have brought us into proximity so that we are not ignorant of the needs of each of our churches, and of the people in our communities. Yet we somehow still find it difficult to cross the barriers that keep us from both transcending our own contexts, and gathering as one community in common witness and service in the world.

When it comes to our divisiveness, how often do we reflect the divisiveness of the world? In truth, how often do we create or re-enforce those divisions? Paul extends a challenge to the church to transcend the usual differentiations between persons in the world. He reminds those in Corinth that for the most part they were not, by the world's standards, persons of stature, nobility, nor even wisdom; they were, in fact, among those the world might consider "foolish": "But God chose what is foolish in the world to shame the wise…" (1: 27). Let us also remember the importance of the cross in Paul's teaching at this point: the cross confounds the usual way of discerning failure or victory.

I would invite us to think about how the concept of the foolishness of the cross challenges us to abandon any boasting about who we are and to what we belong, and calls us to a greater commitment to become the community of faith, undivided in its life as community and in its relationship to the world. The concept of foolishness may, at times, call us to let go of aspects of our lives and of our churches – even some things which, we believe, have developed through faithfulness and wisdom over long years or recently. Are we reminded of the foolishness which is still ours, even as those belonging to community of believers? Are we aware of our foolishness that persists – in defiance of the foolishness of the cross, and the power of the wisdom of God?

Questions for discussion

1. What, in our identities as individuals and churches, reminds us of the foolishness about which Paul writes to the church in Corinth? How might we better respond to Paul's exhortation about the importance of unity?
2. How today might we discern divine wisdom: theologically? practically, in our church life and witness?
3. We are called to be adherents of God's wisdom. How can we witness to our acceptance of this calling?

4. As we read Paul's words about God's wisdom in a hopeless world how might we bear signs of hope through our understanding of the church, and of our participation in God's mission?
5. Where would the cross, wisely understood, lead us as the Christian community today?

NOTE

[1] A key resource for my preparation of this Bible study was Richard B. Hays, *First Corinthians*, Interpretation Commentary Series, Louisville, John Knox, 1997.

V

Sermons

The Search for Unity
The Task of the Church

JOHN W. GLADSTONE

> Now I plead with you, brethren, by the name of our Lord Jesus Christ, that you all speak the same thing, and that there be no divisions among you, but that you be perfectly joined together in the same mind and in the same judgment (1 Cor.1:10).

This exhortation of St Paul expresses his burden of keeping the community of believers in Corinth in unity. For the community of believers in the city of Corinth had *dis*unity among themselves, as he explains only too clearly in this chapter of his letter. The reasons for disunity were the typical reasons, those seen time and again in the life of the church. Paul asks of the community of believers in Corinth: "Is Christ divided? Was *Paul* crucified for you?" (1:13) Thus he appeals strongly for unity.

What Paul indicates here was one of the central problems of the very early church. The Christian community in Corinth must have enjoyed the reputation of being a church in a very wealthy part of the Roman empire, in a city of great cultural heritage. It was also a city of cultural interaction through commercial connections. At the same time, the city was notorious for immorality. Paul had visited this city during his second missionary journey (see Acts 18:1-17). He lived here for about 18 months, and was decisively instrumental in establishing the church. He also had to face stiff opposition from the Jewish population.

After leaving Corinth he comes to know that the church there has several problems, one of them being disunity within the community of believers. Some people claimed to be the disciples of Paul, others those of Apollos, Peter and Christ. Their understanding of leadership and allegiance to certain leaders was a matter on which they differed deeply. Once such differences occur the people involved may be fighting each other, making the church like any other human organization in this world. But this is not what is intended of the people of God. Paul feels immense pain over the unhealthy developments in the church of Corinth,

---

This sermon was delivered at the consultation's opening worship in the Maranathakerk, Driebergen, on 12 September 2002.

and thus he says there should be no divisions among them and they should be of same mind and same judgment.

Later we read that the "spiritual gifts" were another reason for division (see especially 1 Cor. 12:1-11). Culture and tradition would also have augmented these divisions. Perhaps social and economic distinctions, too, might have deepened their disunity. Whatever the reasons for division, the disunity became a "scandal" to the growing church. Therefore Paul exhorts them, saying that they should find their unity in Christ Jesus. The community of believers were joined together in Christ Jesus; this affirmation should enable them to be one in mind and in heart.

For Paul, the authentic teaching of the church should lead to unity in Christ. The apostles and other teachers in the church are only instruments to communicate the message of Christ – or rather, God's instruments to bring the gospel of Christ. Of course the good news of Jesus Christ will have to be proclaimed by people who are called to that ministry. But they cannot be idolized, and must not create "sub-units" or exclusive groups within the community of believers.

There may even have been other reasons which led them to form competing groups within the community of believers, and to fight one another. But the gospel of Christ must transcend all such divisions; those who have accepted the baptism of Christ belong to the people who are united in Jesus Christ. The church is endowed with various gifts; but these gifts must not be a means of disunity. Nor should persons think that there can only be a single gift of the Holy Spirit which is bestowed upon the church: rather, all the gifts are God's blessings towards the building up of the community, which is one in Christ. The church is to be a fellowship, as we read in 1 Corinthians 1:9. Unity is essential to the life of the church.

The church is the body of Christ and the abode of the Holy Spirit. God has called men and women to the fellowship in Jesus Christ; therefore the church is the body of those who are being called by God to live in fellowship. That life, indeed, is the will of God for the people of God. The term "fellowship", or *koinonia*, brings a variety of meanings, all focusing on the relationships among Christians and the churches. Within the ecumenical fellowship, we know much more about *koinonia* as a result of the Faith and Order world conference at Santiago de Compostela in 1993, whose theme was "On the Way to Fuller Koinonia". We know that the church, in its true nature as the people united in Christ, must express its identity through authentic fellowship. Without that it has no credibility: a community of believers which loses its fellowship loses its very nature as a people united in Christ Jesus. For fellowship, *koinonia*, is the essential visible expression of its true nature.

Jesus himself gave much emphasis to the dimension of relationships between and among his followers as a mark of the *new community* which he was founding. In the Sermon on the Mount (in Matt. 5:21-48, to be exact) Jesus uses six illustrations – we often call them antitheses, they have the form "you have heard that it was said... but I say to you" – to illustrate what "righteousness" means. These emphasize the importance the gospel places on the relationship among one another and with God in the new community, the church. God has placed his chosen people as a community – in relation with one another, with God and with God's entire creation. When authentic fellowship was lost in the church in Corinth Paul was pained, and he exhorts the people to foster unity and oneness. For it is in this fellowship that the experience of the kingdom of God will become a reality.

However, Paul knows that this is not an easy task. Once the people are divided, to come back to unity is indeed a very difficult task. So he tells them different ways by which they must try to restore their unity: they have to realize that they are "in Christ Jesus"; that they are called to develop a new consciousness of unity, one that should lead to practising a "common mind" in all aspects of life. All the gifts are of one Spirit; and love should be above every other gift (1 Cor. 12 and 13). So the exhortation of Paul indicates that they should get involved in a search for unity, a search which cannot mean merely doctrinal or academic exercises but something which transforms the life of the people. And this should be the task of the church in and through its growth "into Christ".

We acknowledge that the history of the church is a history of divisions. However, the word of God leads the church with the vision of oneness. Any search for the causes of disunity in the church will surely bring to light social, cultural, political and other factors which have distorted its unity.

Even in countries where the history of Christianity had a comparatively shorter history, the fellowship is broken by disunity. In my part of the world, in India, both older churches and younger churches experience the pain of factions. The serious disunity among some of the older churches creates very serious problems for the witness of the church. At the same time, among the younger churches the communication of the gospel is challenged time and again with denominationalism – leading very often to unhealthy competition. And this is happening just when the life of the church is challenged by the growth of religious fundamentalism.

In the midst of the growing challenges, the true witness to the faith can be imparted only through closer fellowship among various Christian communities. This is also true in several other parts of the world; therefore there is an urgency in the building up of unity within the Christian family. In the midst of all these factors the vision given by the Holy Spirit clearly leads us to participate, with God, in the process of unity. In this we are called to follow him with oneness of mind, knowing that unity is the will of God. This cannot be merely searching here and there; it means following Christ towards the realization of God's will. This is the task given to us, nothing less.

The church is called to overcome all the disuniting factors, to be a community that proclaims the good news of Jesus Christ. The essential task of this community is to give witness in this world. If the church is to be a witnessing community, closer fellowship and oneness are essential. For "doing mission", the unity of the people who confess Jesus Christ as Lord and Saviour is essential. Without an earnest attempt for visible unity, the churches' proclamation becomes less credible.

We must acknowledge that unity is not uniformity. This gives us a vision of unity in which respecting every tradition is to be fostered even as they are brought into closer fellowship. At the same time, the *real* unity will have to be fostered at the level of the people or, rather, at the level of local congregations. We have been experiencing the fact that once the unity is achieved the people enjoy the unity, forgetting all differences of the past. What is needed is the courage to follow God into unity, trusting in him.

God has placed the church in the midst of different kinds of diversities, some of which lead to division. The church, although it is the body of Christ, can also be caught up into these *dis*uniting factors and can be vulnerable to them. Time and again in the life of the church we see that the standards of the world have crept in, creating deep scars in the church's life. Disunity is the ultimate result.

And yet we remember time and again the will for unity, expressed by Jesus Christ himself: "That they all may be one" (John 17:21), and that there shall be "one flock and one shepherd" (John 10:16). Our Lord continues to give his vision, calling us to go forward in the search for unity. This is his will. We must praise God for blessing the human endeavours towards this goal; we have seen marvellous examples of the development of closer fellowship among various denominations. The Christian community is indeed coming closer, and various Christian communities are breaking barriers of disunity and building up new relationships.

We still have to go a long way to go, following our Lord and Saviour Jesus Christ in search of unity and fellowship. But we have come to realize truly, with the experience we have gained across the world, that this movement towards unity is indeed the work of the Holy Spirit. We are brought together by the Holy Spirit to engage in the task given to us by our Lord. All churches, indeed all Christians, who have a common life in Christ are called to grow into a deeper communion, through Christ, with that *koinonia* which is the very life of the trinitarian God in whose image and likeness humanity is created. Therefore all ecclesial communities should make earnest efforts to find agreement on the doctrine of faith, to share the full sacramental life of worship, and to affiliate with one another through a structure which respects their diversity, yet makes their unity visible for all the world to see.

In this search for unity we are being guided by the Holy Spirit. Jesus is with us. He leads us, and we participate with him in this task. The world needs Jesus, and only a church living in unity and fellowship can truly give the true gospel to the world.

Homily on John 21:1-14

JOHN A. RADANO

The central text for this morning's worship is John 21:1-14. The gospel of John is, in a special way, the gospel of the risen Lord. In the Catholic liturgical calendar, the gospel readings for the period immediately following Easter are often taken from the gospel of John.

To me John's gospel is especially the gospel of light – always shedding light on the nature of God. It sheds wondrous light on who Jesus is, as we have seen in the passages from John used at the four early evening worship services these past days: "So the Word became flesh... and we saw his glory, such glory as befits God's only Son..." (John 1:14, on Thursday); "I am the bread of Life" (John 6:35, on Friday); "I am the light of the world" (John 8:12, on Saturday); "I am the resurrection and the life" (John 11:25, on Monday). Perhaps we could add to these, "I am the good Shepherd" (John 10:10) and, "I am the way, the truth and the life" (John 14:6).

John's gospel sheds light on the relation of the Father and the Son ("I am in the Father and the Father is in me...", John 14:10), and their relationship to the Holy Spirit, the Advocate, whom the Father will send in Jesus' name (cf. John 14:26). And in this context, the gospel sheds light on Jesus' expectations for his disciples as he prayed for them: "that they may all be one. As you, Father, are in me and I am in you..." (John 17:21).

Today's passage from John 21 is a post-resurrection story. Jesus appears to the seven disciples who are also fishermen. He meets them where they are, and provokes their faith. He gives them instructions about fishing. They follow his instructions and, while previously unable to catch any fish, now their nets are full. When hauled ashore, the nets, though full, do not break. Jesus himself feeds them. With details such as these, this gospel passage proclaims the risen Christ.

The whole purpose of the ecumenical movement – the whole rationale for separated churches to seek unity, to become Uniting and United

---

This homily was delivered during morning worship on 18 September 2002.

churches – is, finally, so that churches can proclaim together the Risen Lord, that:

He is the light
To him is the glory
His is the victory

The Faith and Order Commission has as its aim "to call the churches to the goal of visible unity in one faith and one eucharistic fellowship, expressed in worship and in common life in Christ".[1] We are still on the way to this goal. Even Uniting and United churches, which have experienced, in some real way, the unity we seek, can recognize that their achievements are still only steps towards the reconciliation of Christ's disciples. Do we still take this goal seriously enough? Do we have the patience needed to pursue this goal? Perhaps in a spirit of prayer we always need to put our doubts, our uncertainties, our achievements and joys, our ecumenical failures and wounds in the hands of the risen Lord who meets his disciples as they are, and where they are.

One of the passages in the Decree on Ecumenism of Vatican II to which I find myself often returning is that passage, in the very first number and paragraph of the decree, which expresses the ecumenical problem and gives the reason for our ecumenical efforts. Referring to the separation among Christians, it says that "their convictions clash and their paths diverge, as though Christ himself were divided (cf. 1 Cor. 1:13)". "This discord openly contradicts the will of Christ, provides a stumbling block to the world, and inflicts damage on the most holy cause of proclaiming the good news to every creature" (*Unitatis Redintegratio*, 1).

What a powerful indictment to our separations: "contradicts the will of Christ", "stumbling block to the world", "inflicts damage on the cause of proclaiming the good news to every creature". To put it in terms of the three major focuses of our consultation this week – unity, mission, identity – this text reminds us that (1) instead of unity there is discord; (2) this discord damages mission, "the most holy cause of proclaiming the good news to every creature", and (3) discord impedes our true identity, prevents us from being identified with the will of Christ, because it contradicts the will of Christ.

Would it not be appropriate when speaking of this discord among Christians to use the word "sin"? Oh, of course today we do not usually speak of our separation from one another as sin. And as we reflect on the role of our ancestors, those who were on different sides of the divide when the separations of Christians took place centuries ago, we would each probably argue that our ancestors did what was right for the sake of the gospel at that time. They were not "sinning". But nonetheless in our ecumenical work for Christian unity, in confronting discord and separation, we are dealing with something which is quite devastating, we can even say: something which is the residue of a sinful result ("it contradicts the will of Christ"), even if those whose actions led to separation had the best of intentions. But, as we know, human nature is often driven by complex, mixed intentions. In working for Christian unity, therefore, we are embracing a noble cause, one which is pleasing to the mind of Christ and, in contrast to division, something responsive to his will.

Verses in today's passage from John 21 bring to mind some significant themes. One thinks of mission, as these fishermen encountered by the risen Lord would become fishers of men and women for Christ, the first missionaries. The text recalls also the tradition which we see elsewhere in the New Testament, that Jesus is recognized in a meal. But something is said in this chapter also in regard to unity. Namely: the "fishermen's net", as we recall, did not break despite the great haul of fish. As one commentator suggests,

> The narrator may here emphasize the fact that the net did not break to point to the unity of these diverse believers in contrast to the divisions over Jesus that had occurred in the unbelieving crowd (in previous chapters of the gospel, e.g. chapters 7:43; 9:16; 10:19).[2]

If this is the case, in order to underscore how devastating our divisions are and how noble is the work for Christian unity, perhaps we can give some freedom here to our imagination. Can you join me in imagining now, tongue in cheek, an apocryphal scene structured along the lines of today's gospel text? Imagine a scene in which the risen Lord appears to other disciples some centuries later, after they have separated from one another, after the schism in the 11th century and the breakdown of Western Christianity after the 16th century.

Unlike Peter and his companions these later, separated followers of Christ, our more recent ancestors, would have gone out fishing in separate boats, not one boat. At Jesus' instruction, those in each separate boat would have thrown a net on the side of their own boat, so that each boat could bring its separate haul of fish (perhaps in this case their nets would break). And perhaps Jesus, respecting our freedom to be what we are, would have set up several separate fires on the shore and would share separate meals with separate groups. He would want it to be otherwise, he would want them to be one; but because they are free, he would work with the reality that exists. He would again meet the disciples where and as they are.

At the same time the risen Lord would invite them – us – to overcome divergences (as compared with legitimate diversity) so that when he made a future appearance, perhaps in some future century, presuming that they – we – respond to the grace of the Spirit and that our ecumenical work is successful, there would be again only one boat, one fire, and one meal which all could share, all together with the risen Lord.

This week we have heard many realities – not apocryphal stories – about United and Uniting churches. We have heard about significant recent developments in the Netherlands, South Africa, India, the United States, to name some places. But we have also heard that these church union movements take many years. Those involved struggle over many issues. We have seen that it is easy to be discouraged, to wonder if any real progress is being made. It is like the disciples, the fishermen, in today's gospel passage, who put their nets overboard, but at first caught nothing. We can easily wonder if our ecumenical efforts will achieve anything, at least in our life-time.

Yet when we stop to review the progress, as we do in a meeting like this, we realize, too, that even with all the difficulties (past, present and, no doubt, to come), progress continues to be made. There have been important achievements. Perhaps, in fact, as he did with the disciples by the Sea of Tiberias, the risen Lord has met his disciples where they are, in the midst of their ecumenical struggles. Perhaps the impulse to throw the nets out once again, to rise up and take the ecumenical task by the horns, and to have the energy to go forward in face of difficulties, has come from him. For, in fact, important things have been achieved.

I would like to mention here the example of the Joint Declaration on the Doctrine of Justification signed on 31 October 1999 by officials of the Lutheran World Federation and the Catholic Church. It states, in regard to justification – the issue which, we recall, was at the heart of the conflict between Martin Luther and the church authorities in the 16th century, the issue at the heart of the Reformation, the issue which, in a sense, symbolized the reasons for the divisions among Christians which began then and have continued up to now – that "the understanding of the doctrine of justification set forth in this Declaration shows that a consensus in basic truths of the doctrine of justification exists between Lutherans and Catholics" (no. 40). And thus, the doctrinal condemnations of the 16th century relating to the doctrine of justification do not apply to the teaching of the Catholic Church or of the Lutheran churches as presented in this declaration (cf. no. 41).

It took some forty years of patient dialogue to arrive at this declaration, including periods of time when it was not clear whether this goal could be achieved, periods of time when it seemed that "the fish were not biting", times perhaps when, to the scholars and ecumenists whose vision was that a major step towards unity was in reach, it may all have seemed in vain. I ask myself whether, at those dry times, it was not the risen Lord who was there, quietly, to encourage those ecumenists to try again, to cast the nets once more into the sea with the hope that there might, this time, be a result. Because, in fact, there were results. There were big results. The Joint Declaration is a major achievement. Although full communion between Lutherans and Catholics has not yet been achieved, the Joint Declaration helps them to confess, better than ever before, together before the world the saving action of Jesus Christ.

The "bottom line" is that we engage in ecumenical work in order that eventually we will be able, together, to praise the risen Lord. We seek unity so that eventually we will be able, together, without the obstacle of separation, to witness to the risen Lord, and together share in his mission of salvation. We seek unity so that some day we can all share the sacred meal of the Risen Lord, together.

Let us pray for one another today. Let us pray for United and Uniting churches. Let us pray for the strength to continue the pilgrimage towards unity. Let us praise the Risen Lord in the spirit of the verse from the hymn used in this morning's worship:

Thine be the glory,
Risen conquering Son
Endless is the victory
Thou o'er death has won.[3]

Amen.

NOTES

[1] By-laws of the Faith and Order Commission, Aim and Functions, 3.1; see *Faith and Order in Moshi: The 1996 Commission Meeting*, Alan Falconer ed., Faith and Order Paper no. 177, WCC Publications, 1998, p.323.

[2] Pheme Perkins, "The Gospel According to John", in *The New Jerome Biblical Commentary*, Raymond E. Brown, SS, Joseph A. Fitzmeyer, SJ, Roland E. Murphy, O.Carm. eds, Englewood Cliffs, Prentice-Hall, 1990, p.985.

[3] Words: Edmond L. Budry, 1904, trans. R. Birch Hoyle, 1923; Music: George Friedrich Händel, 1746.

The Imperative of Unity

BAS PLAISIER

First scripture reading: Ezekiel 37:15-23

Join the two sticks together into one stick, so that they may become one… they shall be my people, and I will be their God…

Second scripture reading: 1 Corinthians 2:1-5

With a demonstration of the Spirit and of power…

Third scripture reading: 1 Peter 2:4-10

Let yourselves be built into a spiritual house, to be a holy priesthood... [to] proclaim the mighty acts of him who called you out of darkness into his marvellous light...

Brothers and sisters,

Is it necessary? Necessary to become one body?

Why are some of the biblical writers so obsessed with unity? Why are they deeply moved by the vision of the one people: one, whether Jews or Christians? Why, for them, is the joining of several parts together in one body so important?

In Dutch society we hardly ever see such a passion for unity anymore. To join church organizations together in one church has, generally speaking, no priority. Many Christians have lost their faith in unity, possibly as a result of the forty-years-journey of the three "Together on the Way" churches or – and I guess that is the main reason – due to the lack of belief in the benefit of structures and supra-local organizations. Almost every Dutch Christian might acknowledge the "oikoumene of the heart", the spiritual unity between believers; but often they don't act to bring together all their Christian friends together in one congregation or one church...

I guess many members of the churches would like to ask the apostle Paul: Is it helpful to emphasize the sin of diversity? Isn't it true that multiformity and diversity are wonderful gifts of our God? We all are unique, all people are different: don't try to ignore that! "Don't try to reach the impossible, Paul..."

This sermon was delivered at the consultation's closing worship held in the Morgensterkapel, Driebergen, 18 September 2002.

And what about Jesus' prayer for unity in John 17?

How many times we have quoted these marvellous words? But we have also tried to shift their meaning in *our* "direction": Yes, we would like to be one: spiritually. Yes, we emphasize the unity – but not without the truth.

We try to understand Jesus in his own time: for a small group, quarrels and struggles are disastrous. Twelve persons *have* to be as one.

But is it real, does it make any sense, to aspire to a unity with 100 or 1000 people?

You have probably heard the joke of the Dutch: one Dutchman means a theologian; two Dutchmen, then we have a church. And with three – two churches are coming up...

That is our context here in the Netherlands, but I guess also in many other countries. We like to hear about unity; and sometimes we are very serious in our prayer for it. We also dare to emphasize the sin of separatism, and the reality of the abundance of churches... But most of the time, our talk about unity has become a liturgical phrase, a Christian mantra, without consequences for our church programmes.

However, we hear the prophet Ezekiel

He tells us about a revelation and a vision: the vision of God. It is the Lord who speaks to him about the unity of the two separate parts of Israel: Judah and Joseph. And then Ezekiel starts his walk in the city. In his hands he holds two sticks, with the names of the separate parts of Israel: Judah and Joseph.

Two sticks as an image of their situation of division.

In former times they were one nation under God. But they experienced the painful history of division and split. Gradually they grew apart from each other. Time didn't heal the wounds – on the contrary! The division became the normal situation, unity was abnormal.

The Lord, however, didn't forget his original election of *one* nation; his original purpose with Israel. It should be one nation in obedience to the words of God, and with the task of glorifying God's name, and demonstrating the will of God in righteousness and shalom. Unity means "they will not defile themselves with idols or corrupt themselves with sin..."

Unity is the ultimate goal of God to demonstrate his love and holiness

Unity also means for the two nations: reconciliation and conversion and purification. The prophet has to bind the two sticks together to make one stick.

This doesn't mean a continuation of the sinful past, but a new beginning of their relation with God and with their brothers and sisters...

Uniting churches into one church will only succeed when, beyond the continuity of the structures of the past, there is a new longing to shape a *new* structure.

Is it possible?

"I will purify them, they will be my people, and I will be their God"

That is the promise of God. Unity is a task, but also a gift of God. In the unity of one nation – of one church – our Lord God will demonstrate his presence and lead us in the truth and the unity of faith.

God will unite two nations. He will do it, and he promises his presence.

I hear in these words the passion of God for unity. Why is he so passionate? It is true: our Lord also created the diversity and the colourful multiformity. But his ultimate goal is unity.

Because *He is one*.

And the shape of that nation – the shape of the church – shows his Oneness, and his essential will of reconciliation and love. His love is not divided and confused. His word for the world is not "yes and no", or "a contradiction in itself". Our Lord is faithful, and thus his people have to be faithful and have to live from one source. Therefore Ezekiel bound the two sticks and joined them together.

This is the background of the apostle Paul's passion for unity in the first epistle to the Corinthians. "Is Christ divided?" (1 Cor. 1:13) Or – with other words – isn't it impossible, and shameful, to resign oneself to division and the "reality" of divided churches? The *koinonia* with Jesus Christ implies the *koinonia* with the brothers and sisters, and with the other parts of the body of Christ. I hear in these emotional words the echo of the voice of the Lord to Ezekiel.

The words say: Don't put up with the so-called "normal" situation of division and internal quarrels between churches.

I know these words are not easy, and also not in accordance with the usual thinking in our churches and society in Europe. In fact we think we don't *need* the Holy Spirit who is the bond of peace.

Paul said that he didn't come with big words and great learnings – he just came according to the needs of the Corinthians. He came to them to glorify Jesus Christ, to preach the gospel of the crucified and risen Lord.

And in the light of this Saviour we see only one body. And we will preach this gospel. And we will emphasize, each and every time, that unity is not shaped according to people's thoughts today, but is the word and the promise of God.

Paul was preaching "with a demonstration of the Spirit and of power" (1 Cor. 2:4)

Paul's action was the same as Ezekiel's: the "reality" in each situation was the division of God's people; the promise was: God's word and God's power.

The reality is our slowness and unbelief in God's promises; but the vision is the unity of the body of Christ.

Our task is to bind what is separated and to join it together

Our task is: to act and preach in the power of the Spirit and – in the words of Peter: to build the temple of God with living stones.

This is for me, and for many of the members of our churches, the power and the hope to continue with the Protestant Church in the Netherlands – because that will be our name after the union in 2004. Sometimes in the past, it seemed impossible and unreal to persevere in our belief of visible unity in one Protestant church. But God is faithful, and he fulfilled his promises – and gave us the power to maintain our vision and to go forward, step-by-step.

Why?

Because He called us and showed us the way to unity, and to a church which will proclaim the wonderful acts of God, who called us out of darkness into God's own marvellous light.

Brothers and sisters, let us celebrate this! Let us celebrate the unity in Christ, the unity of all God's people in the world.

God is faithful: He will bring us together in the fellowship of his Son, Jesus Christ our Lord. Amen.

Participants

Italics = organization represented
Parentheses = church affiliation, when not otherwise clear

Rev. Francis Amenu
England, United Kingdom
((Evangelical) Presbyterian Church, Ghana)
Ghanaian Ministry for London/ United Reformed Church

Rev. Dr Thomas F. Best
Switzerland / U.S.A.
(Christian Church (Disciples of Christ))
Faith and Order / WCC staff

Prof. J. P. Boendermaker
Netherlands
(Evangelical Lutheran Church in the Kingdom of the Netherlands) [Uniting Protestant Churches in the Netherlands])
Lutheran World Federation

Kirchenrätin Ursula Brecht
Germany
(Evangelical Church of the Church Province of Saxony)
Arnoldshain Conference

Rev. Prof. Dr Martien Brinkman
Netherlands
(Reformed Churches in the Netherlands [Uniting Protestant Churches in the Netherlands])
Vrije Universiteit, Faculty of Theology

Rev. Dionito M. Cabillas
Philippines
Philippine Independent Church

Bishop Erme Camba
Philippines
United Church of Christ in the Philippines/Commission on World Mission and Evangelism, WCC

Rev. J. Patrick Coltman
Republic of South Africa
United Congregational Church of Southern Africa/Church Unity Commission (CUC)

Rev. Terence Corkin
Australia
Uniting Church in Australia

Rev. Dr David Cornick
England, United Kingdom
United Reformed Church

Dr Peter Cruchley-Jones
Wales, United Kingdom
United Reformed Church

Ms Jet Den Hollander
Switzerland
(Uniting Protestant Churches in the Netherlands)
Mission in Unity Project, World Alliance of Reformed Churches

Rev. Mario A. Dos Santos
Angola
United Evangelical Church – Anglican Communion in Angola

Rt Rev.Dr John W. Gladstone
India
Anglican Communion / Church of South India

Dr Eddy Hallewas
Netherlands
(Evangelical Lutheran Church in the Kingdom of the Netherlands) [Uniting Protestant Churches in the Netherlands])
Lutheran World Federation

Rev. Dr Sint Kimhachandra
Thailand
Church of Christ in Thailand

Rev. Dr Michael Kinnamon
USA
(Christian Church (Disciples of Christ))
Churches Uniting in Christ

Rev. Prof. Dr Leo J. Koffeman
Netherlands
(Reformed Churches in the Netherlands [Uniting Protestant Churches in the Netherlands])
"Together on the Way" Churches

Oberkirchenrätin Cordelia Kopsch
Germany
(Evangelical Church in Hessen and Nassau)
Arnoldshain Conference

Kirchenrätin Susanne Labsch
Germany
(Protestant Church in Baden)
Evangelical Church in Germany

Rev. Canon John Lindsay
Scotland, United Kingdom
Scottish Episcopal Church

Rt Rev. Dr Isaac Mar Philoxenos
India
Mar Thoma Syrian Church of Malabar

Mrs Rachel Mathew
India
(Mar Thoma Syrian Church of Malabar)
Communion of Churches in India

Rev. Sheila Maxey
England, United Kingdom
United Reformed Church

Mrs Carolyn McComish
Switzerland / England
Protestant Church of Geneva
Faith and Order / WCC staff

Prof. Piet G. Meiring
South Africa
Dutch Reformed Church [South Africa]

Rt Rev. B.D. Mondal
Bangladesh
Church of Bangladesh

Rev. Dr Hiroshi Omiya
Japan
United Church of Christ in Japan

Archimandrite Athenagoras Peckstadt
Belgium
Ecumenical Patriarchate

Rev. Dr Jerry Pillay
South Africa
Uniting Presbyterian Church in Southern Africa/Church Unity Commission (CUC)

Mgr John Radano
Vatican City
Pontifical Council for Promoting Christian Unity, Roman Catholic Church

Dr David Ross
Aotearoa-New Zealand
(Presbyterian Church of New Zealand)
Forum of Cooperative Ventures

Rt Rev. Dr D.K. Sahu
India
Church of North India

Rt Rev. Thomas Samuel
India
Church of South India

Mr Hans Schravesande
Netherlands
(Uniting Protestant Churches in the Netherlands)
Council for World Mission

Rev. Thomas Seville, CR
England, United Kingdom
Church of England

Mrs Ann Shillaker
Wales, United Kingdom
(United Reformed Church)
ENFYS: The Covenanted Churches in Wales

Rev. Silishebo Silishebo
Zambia
United Church of Zambia

Rev. Johannes Sindano
Namibia
Evangelical Lutheran Church in Namibia

Rev. Norbert Stephens
Jamaica, WI
United Church in Jamaica and the Cayman Islands

Rev. Dr David M. Thompson
England, United Kingdom
(United Reformed Church)
Disciples Ecumenical Consultative Council

Rev. Ian Thompson
Scotland, United Kingdom
(Church of Scotland)
Scottish Church Initiative for Union (SCIFU)

Rev. Lydia Veliko
USA
United Church of Christ/ Ecumenical Partnership Disciples/UCC

Rev. Dr Robert Welsh
USA
Christian Church (Disciples of Christ)/ Ecumenical PartnershipDisciples/UCC/ Disciples Ecumenical Consultative Council

Sister Eluned Williams, MBE
Wales, United Kingdom
(Methodist Church, Wales)
ENFYS: The Covenanted Churches in Wales

Rev. Dr Bertrice Wood
USA
Churches Uniting in Christ (CUIC)

Rev. Marek Zikmund
Czech Republic
Evangelical Church of Czech Brethren

Rev. Londi Zulu
Republic of South Africa
Methodist Church of Southern Africa/ Church Unity Commission (CUC)

Contributors

Rev. Francis Amenu (Evangelical Presbyterian Church, Ghana) is minister of the Ghanaian Ministry for London.

Rev. Dr Thomas F. Best, a pastor of the Christian Church (Disciples of Christ), is executive secretary for Faith and Order, World Council of Churches.

Rev. Prof. Dr Martien E. Brinkman (Reformed Churches in the Netherlands [Uniting Protestant Churches in the Netherlands]) is a Reformed theologian and professor of ecumenical theology at the Vrije Universiteit in Amsterdam, Netherlands.

Rev. Terence Corkin is general secretary of The Uniting Church in Australia.

Rev. Dr Peter Cruchley-Jones (United Reformed Church) is in full-time pastoral ministry in Cardiff, Wales. He teaches mission at St Michael's College, Cardiff and is also an honorary research associate of the religious studies and theology department of Cardiff University.

Rt Rev. Dr John W. Gladstone is bishop of the South Kerala diocese, Church of South India.

Ms Jet den Hollander is a lay member of the Uniting Protestant Churches in the Netherlands and the executive secretary of the Mission in Unity Project, a joint programme of the World Alliance of Reformed Churches and the John Knox International Reformed Centre in Geneva, Switzerland.

Rev. Prof. Dr Leo J. Koffeman (Reformed Churches in the Netherlands [Uniting Protestant Churches in the Netherlands]) is ecumenical officer of the Uniting Protestant Churches in the Netherlands, and teaches church law and ecumenism at Kampen Theological University. From 1 July 2004 he will serve part-time as ecumenical staff for the Protestant

Church in the Netherlands, and (in addition to teaching at Kampen) will be associate professor for church law at the Theological Academic Institute serving the Universities of Utrecht and Leiden.

Rev. Dr Michael Kinnamon (Christian Church (Disciples of Christ)), former general secretary of the Consultation on Church Union, is Allen and Dottie Miller professor of mission and peace at Eden Theological Seminary, St Louis, MO, USA.

(Rev. Dr) Prof. P.G.J. (Piet) Meiring (Dutch Reformed Church, South Africa) serves on the staff of the faculty of theology, University of Pretoria, South Africa.

Rev. Dr Jerry Pillay is minister at St Andrew's Uniting Presbyterian Church, Benoni, South Africa, and moderator-designate of the Uniting Presbyterian Church in Southern Africa (to assume office in September 2004). He is convener of the priorities and resources committee and member of the ecumenical relations committee of the church's general assembly.

Rev. Dr Bas Plaisier (Netherlands Reformed Church [Uniting Protestant Churches in the Netherlands]) has served from June 1997 as general secretary of the Uniting Churches in the Netherlands. From 1 May 2004 he will be general secretary of the Protestant Church in the Netherlands.

Msgr John A. Radano is head of the Western Section of the Pontifical Council for Promoting Christian Unity, Vatican City, Europe.

Rt Rev. Dr D.K. Sahu is bishop of the diocese of Eastern Himalaya, Church of North India.

Rev. Norbert D. Stephens (United Church in Jamaica and the Cayman Islands) is pastor of the Webster memorial United Church, Jamaica W.I.

Rev. Dr David M. Thompson (United Reformed Church, UK) is reader in modern church history at the University of Cambridge, director of the Centre for Advanced Religious and Theological Studies, and president of Fitzwilliam College. He is also moderator of the Disciples' Ecumenical Consultative Council, and a long-standing member of the Disciples of Christ-Roman Catholic International Dialogue.

Rev. Dr Bertrice Y. Wood (United Church of Christ, USA) is director of Churches Uniting in Christ [USA].